badak
rhinoceros

Selamat belajar. Sampai jumpa.
Have fun learning! See you soon!

uang
money

es kelapa muda
young coconut water

perkawinan Islam di Jawa
an Islamic wedding in Java

pelangi
rainbow

penari Bali
Balinese dancer

penjual jamu
herbal drinks seller

**The free online audio recordings for this book
may be downloaded as follows:**

Type the following URL into your web browser:
www.tuttlepublishing.com/Indonesian-Picture-Dictionary
For support, email us at info@tuttlepublishing.com

INDONESIAN
PICTURE
DICTIONARY

LEARN MORE THAN 1,500 INDONESIAN WORDS AND EXPRESSIONS

Linda Hibbs

TUTTLE Publishing

Tokyo | Rutland, Vermont | Singapore

Contents

A Basic Introduction to the Indonesian Language

Each ethnic group in Indonesia has its own language and in many cases several different languages are spoken on different parts of one island. The people of West Java, for example, speak Sundanese which is different from the Javanese spoken in Central Java and East Java.

So that everyone can communicate and understand each other, an 'Indonesian language' called *Bahasa Indonesia* was created as the national language in 1928. It was first introduced into schools in the 1950s.

The basis of this national language is the Malay language and it incorporates words from local languages (in particular Javanese), as well as words that are borrowed from Sanskrit, Arabic, Portuguese, Chinese, Dutch and later English, due to their influence on Indonesia historically. As the colonial rulers of Indonesia for 300 years, the Dutch often used the Malay language for administration and treaties and introduced it as a language of education in the late nineteenth century.

As it is the language of a dynamic, modern nation, the lexicon of *Bahasa Indonesia* continues to expand along with its grammatical structures and idiomatic usages. So whilst some may assume the language is the same as Malay, it is in fact now quite different. *Bahasa Indonesia* is the official language of government, education, business and the media. Regional languages, colloquial expressions and the dialect of Jakarta continue to be popular in everyday interactions, and they all contribute to the richness of the national language. Indonesians often speak several languages—their own regional language, the national language and some English. Local languages are taught in primary and Junior secondary schools alongside *Bahasa Indonesia*.

Formal or Informal language

The language spoken in Indonesia often depends on whether the situation is formal or informal. Speaking to someone older than yourself , for example, requires more formal language. Speaking amongst those of a similar age will include colloquialisms.

Written Indonesian is more formal and will often include passive structure, which is explained later. You should be aware of these differences. Safer to err on the side of formal than informal if you are not sure.

Pronunciation and syllable stress

Unlike Javanese and many other Asian languages, Indonesian does not have its own script. It is a romanized phonetic language, which is written using the Latin alphabet and is spelled as it sounds. However, watch out for the various pronunciations of '**e**' (listen carefully to the audio), and the letter '**c**' which is pronounced as '*ch*'; for example, **cicak** (a gecko) is pronounced *chi-chak* (the '**k**' at the end is almost silent.)

In Indonesian, syllables receive almost equal stress but with slight emphasis on the second or second to last syllable, especially if there are more than two syllables in a word. For example, **selamat**: *se-la-mat* or **bersekolah**: *ber-se-ko-lah*.

Other specific sounds that identify Indonesian are the soft vowel sounds, the rolling of the '**r**', the '**au**' and '**ai**' sounds, the '**ng**' sound and as mentioned above, the '**k**' at the end of some words that is almost not heard (a glottal stop).

Spelling

If you use other resources including the Internet, or you find yourself in Indonesia when reading this dictionary, you will occasionally notice some differences in spelling. This is partly because certain letters in the spelling system were changed in the 1970s (eg. 'tj' is now 'c', 'dj' is now 'j', 'j' is now 'y') and also because some words borrowed from English, Dutch, Arabic or other languages can have alternate spellings closer to the original (for example **jaman** or **zaman**, which comes from Arabic and means "era").

The Indonesian alphabet has 26 letters which are pronounced as follows:

A	B	C	D	E	F	G	H	I	J	K	L	M
ah	beh	cheh	deh	eh	ef	geh	ha	ee	jey	kah	el	em

N	O	P	Q	R	S	T	U	V	W	X	Y	Z
en	oh	peh	kee	air	ess	teh	oo	feh	weh	iks	ye-ee	zet

Knowing how the alphabet is pronounced is not essential but helps when you have to spell out your name and to refer to things such as '**WC**' (Water Closet pronounced '**Weh-cheh**' a popular term for toilet) or '**AC**' (aircon) pronounced '**Ah-cheh**'.

This book does not aim to provide a full introduction to Indonesian grammar. The phrases presented do not include any of the more complex structures. There are, however, a few grammatical characteristics that you will notice as you learn the vocabulary.

- word order (the main difference from English is that modifiers come after nouns they modify)
- pronouns (informal and formal pronouns)
- no direct word for 'is' or 'are'
- prefixes and suffixes are frequently attached to base words to form new words
- time indicators (verbs do not indicate tense so time words are added)
- frequent use of 'passive' sentence structures instead of 'active' verb forms
- no gender or plural forms of nouns or adjectives

Word order and simple sentence structure

Basic sentence word order is the same as in English (subject + verb + object):

Dia membaca buku.   He/she reads books; he/she reads a book.

However, possessives, adjectives and other descriptive terms come after the nouns they modify:

Nama saya Alicia.   My name is Alicia. (My name = nama saya)
Nama teman saya Max.   My friend's name is Max. (My friend's name = Nama teman saya)
Rumah saya.   My house.
Rumah baru ini.   This new house.

Pronouns

Pronouns in Indonesian are important and using the polite forms of these or avoiding them altogether is part of learning to communicate in the language.

	FORMAL	INFORMAL
1st person:	*saya*—I/my	*aku*—I/my
		ku—short for *aku* and used as possesive 'my'

kami—we/our/us (not including the person you are speaking to)
kita—we/our/us (including the person you are speaking to)

	FORMAL	INFORMAL
2nd person	***Anda***—you/your (more formal and replaces a name, hence capital letter)	***kamu***—you/your (familiar, equal status or lower) ***mu***—short for *kamu* (possesive)
	ibu mum; mother; respectful term of address for women (like 'Madam' or 'Mrs' in English)	
	bapak dad; father; respectful term of address for men (like 'Sir' or 'Mr' in English)	
	kalian; sekalian plural (you all)	
3rd person	***dia***—he/she; his/her; him/her	
	-nya (added to end of word)—his/her/its	
	mereka—they/their/them	

The word ***kamu***, should only be used to address friends or family. If you are not sure you can use the person's name if you know it, or if they are older, ***Ibu (Bu)*** or ***Bapak (Pak)***.

The word ***Mas*** (particularly in Java) is a respectful term of address for someone of a similar age and is also used when speaking to service staff such as *becak* drivers or a waiter in a restaurant. ***Mbak*** is the female equivalent.

The word ***Anda*** with a capital A, has in more recent years been adopted as a word that is polite and can be used in situations for you or your. This is more often used in advertisements.

No specific word for 'is' or 'are'

There are no specific words for is/are in Indonesian. Sometimes the word ***adalah*** is used to link two parts of a sentence.

> For example:
> ***Jalan Malioboro adalah jalan rayanya kota Yogyakarta.***
> Malioboro street is the main street of Yogyakarta.

It is not used in most situations where we use 'is', however.

That dog (is) big.	He (is) a teacher.	This (is) my house.
Anjing itu besar.	***Dia guru.***	***Ini rumah saya.***

Prefixes and suffixes

Many Indonesian words are formed by adding prefixes and suffixes to base words. This is especially true of verbs. There are three basic active verb forms; 1) Simple (no affixes) 2) with ***ber-*** added and 3) with ***me-*** added (with or without suffixes *-i* or *-kan*). Note that ***ber-*** and ***me-*** are often dropped.

Simple verbs

makan ⇒ to eat   *Dia makan apel.* He is eating an apple/He eats an apple.
minum ⇒ to drink   *Saya suka minum kopi.* I like to drink coffee.
tinggal ⇒ to live   *Saya tinggal di Jakarta.* I live in Jakarta.
tidur   ⇒ to sleep   *Saya tidur pada jam sepuluh malam.* I go to sleep at 10pm.

ber- verbs
(base)

main ⇒ ***bermain*** = to play
kerja ⇒ ***bekerja*** = to work
asal ⇒ ***berasal*** = to originate from

6

Some verbs can be created by adding **ber**- to a noun:

sekolah ⇒ school	**bersekolah**	=	to go to school
sepeda ⇒ bike	**bersepeda**	=	to go by bike
nama ⇒ name	**bernama**	=	to have the name (be called)

Me- verbs

The formation of **me**- verbs depends on what consonant or vowel the word begins with. Sometimes the first letter of the base word has to be dropped (makes it easier to pronounce).

Prefix	Used before	Example
me-	l, m, n, r, w	*lihat* ⇒ *melihat*
mem-	b, f, p (dropped)	*pakai* ⇒ *memakai*
men-	c, d, j, t (dropped)	*jual* ⇒ *menjual*
meng-	a, e, i, o, u, g, h, k (dropped)	*kenal* ⇒ *mengenal*
meny-	s (dropped)	*simpan* ⇒ *menyimpan*

Prefixes and suffixes are used to create new words

Example:		
	main	⇒ to play
	bermain	⇒ to play
	bermain-main	⇒ to play around/fool about
	memainkan	⇒ to play something (a record or a role)
	mempermainkan	⇒ to manipulate, make a fool of someone
	mainan	⇒ toy
	pemain	⇒ player/actor
	permainan	⇒ a game

Importance of time indicators (verbs do not indicate past or future tense)

Time is not indicated by changing the form of the verb like it is in many European languages. Time words are added instead. So instead of 'eat', 'ate' or 'will eat', time is expressed by using specific time words such as:

besok	tomorrow or sometime in the future
kemarin	yesterday
kemarin dulu	previous to yesterday
dulu	sometime in the past
hari ini	today
nanti	sometime soon (later)
tadi	just now; earlier (eg. **tadi pagi** = earlier this morning)

Example: **Dia _duduk_ di samping jendela.**   She is sitting/sits by the window. (present)

Kemarin dia _duduk_ di samping jendela.   Yesterday she sat by the window. (past)

Object focus or "passive" structure

Indonesians often prefer to emphasize the object or the outcome of an action rather than the person or thing that is involved in the action. This is called passive sentence structure where more focus is placed on the object (what is being talked about) by placing it first and less focus on the subject (the speaker or the one doing the action) which follows. This is not commonly used in English. The passive structure is probably one of the hardest things to grasp when learning Indonesian. If you can remember that it is basically to focus on the object coming first, and to take away the focus of the person, it will start to make more sense.

The first example below is an 'active sentence'. The emphasis is on the person doing the action (Amir). The second example is a 'passive sentence' where the book is now the focus.

Amir membaca buku itu.
Amir is reading that book

Buku itu dibaca Amir.
That book is being read by Amir

Note that the verb in the passive sentence has changed from **membaca** to **dibaca**. This is used when it is third person (in this case a name). The verb does not change with other pronouns but the word order is different as you can see from the samples below.

First person: **Active**: *Saya membaca buku itu.* (I am reading that book.)
                  Passive: *Buku itu saya baca.*

Second person: **Active**: *Kami sudah membaca buku itu.* (We have already read that book.)
                  Passive: *Buku itu sudah kami baca.*

Third person: **Active**: *Dia membaca buku itu.* (He is reading that book.)
                  Passive: *Buku itu sudah dibacanya.*
                  Buku itu sudah dibaca (oleh) mereka.
                  Buku itu sudah dibaca (oleh) Joko/siswa itu.

Passive constructions are often used without a subject being mentioned. The sentences below show this.

Active (Subject Focus = person is the focus):   *Bapak menjual buah-buahan segar di pasar.*
                                                    Father sells fresh fruit at the market.
Passive (Object Focus = the object is the focus ie. the fruit):
                                                    Buah-buahan segar dijualnya di pasar.
                                                    Fresh fruit is sold (by) him at the market.
and frequently used: *Buah-buahan segar dijual di pasar.*
                                                    Fresh fruit is sold at the market.
                                                    (no specific subject is given)

Plurals

Plural in Indonesian is indicated by the context. In the past the word was sometimes duplicated and whilst you may occasionally see this in written form, and with certain words such as **bumbu-bumbu** (spices), it is not commonly used.

Apel ini merah. This apple is red.
Dia membeli apel di pasar. She/he buys apples at the market.

Language and culture are integral to the identity of a person and it is important to understand the context in which the language is formed and used. For this reason, this Indonesian picture dictionary introduces themes and words relevant to Indonesian cultural and social settings which can be used by learners in any situation. The images acccompanying each word or phrase are meant to offer an insight into the context in which the words and phrases might be used as well as to present a visual image of the diversity of life in Indonesia.

The goal of this picture dictionary is to teach vocabulary based around themes and to include the simple grammar that has been introduced in this introduction through sentences and conversations relevant to the vocabulary. The dictionary may be approached topically, choosing a theme and then learning all the words surrounding that topic. However, some themes build on others and as a result some of the vocabulary presented in later themes includes vocabulary from earlier themes, thus giving you the opportunity to put your prior learned knowledge to use.

This dictionary aims to show a selection of both formal and informal language but leans more towards formal as this is essential to learn in order to write and speak and understand Indonesian in any given setting. A dictionary like this, however, cannot cover all grammatical explanations or examples nor more elaborate discussion. But it can be a launching pad for furthering your own discussions and interactions.

For those of you who are hoping to improve your Indonesian vocabulary skills, this dictionary is ideal. The thematic nature of the sections allows you to learn new words as well as to review ones you may already be familiar with. For review, you can dive in and out of any theme in the book quickly.

The free online audio recordings by native Indonesian speakers provide accurate pronunciations for all the words, sentences and conversations found in the book, and students should use these to practice their pronunciation. A link to download the recordings is given here.

**The free online audio recordings for this book
may be downloaded as follows:**

Type the following URL into your web browser:
www.tuttlepublishing.com/Indonesian-Picture-Dictionary
For support, email us at info@tuttlepublishing.com

Apa kabar?
How are you?

1 **Halo, apa kabar?**
Hello, how are you?

2 **Baik–baik saja!**
I am fine, thank you!

3 **bertemu**
to meet

4 **Kenalkan, ini teman saya Hasan.**
Let me introduce my friend Hasan.

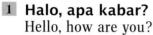
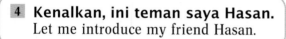

8 **Selamat pagi**
Good morning
(up to midday)

9 **Selamat siang**
Good day
(noon up to 3pm)

10 **Selamat sore**
Good afternoon
(from 3pm to 6pm)

11 **Selamat malam**
Good-night/evening

12 **Ayo!**
Come on! Let's go!*
*It is polite to face the palm downwards when calling someone to come toward you.

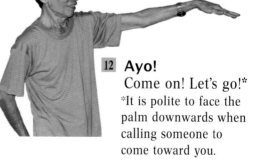

5 **Halo!**
Hello!

7 **berkenalan**
getting to know someone

6 **Senang berkenalan denganmu, Hasan.**
Pleased to meet you, Hasan.

13 **Sampai jumpa lagi.**
Until we meet again.

14 Hai, nama saya Andre. Siapa nama Anda?
Hi, my name is Andre. What's your name?

15 Nama saya Carol. Ini kartu nama saya.
My name is Carol. This is my name/business card.

16 **menyambut**
to greet (receive)

17 **memperkenalkan diri**
to introduce yourself

---

18 **Selamat tinggal!**
Good-bye! (said by the person leaving to the people staying)

19 **Selamat jalan...**
Good-bye... (said by the people staying behind)
Sampai besok.
Until tomorrow.

20 **pertemuan**
gathering; meeting

Additional Vocabulary

24 **nama**
name

25 **nama keluarga**
family name

26 **Anda**
you (polite)

27 **kenal**
to know (s.o.)

28 **bersalaman**
to shake hands

29 **selamat tinggal**
good-bye
("safe stay" to those staying)

30 **selamat jalan**
good-bye
("safe journey" to someone leaving)

31 **ini**
this

32 **itu**
that

33 **jumpa**
to meet

34 **sampai bertemu lagi**
until we meet again

35 **saya pergi dulu**
I'll be going now (to take one's leave)

36 **Bagaimana kabarnya?**
How are things going?

37 **teman**
friends

38 **pulang**
return home

39 **salam**
greeting

40 **pergi**
to go

41 **selamat**
safe (used in greetings)

21 **Terima kasih!**
Thank you!

23 **tamu**
guest; visitor

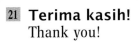

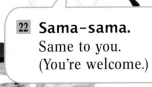

22 **Sama-sama.**
Same to you.
(You're welcome.)

2 Keluarga saya
My family

1 orangtua
parents

2 anak
child

3 pria **4 wanita**
male female

5 anak laki-laki
son

6 anak perempuan
daughter

7 anak-anak
children

Additional Vocabulary

25 keluarga
family

26 laki-laki
man

27 perempuan
woman

28 ibu (bu)
mother (Mrs.)

29 bapak (pak)
father (Mr.)

30 cucu
grandson;
granddaughter

31 istri
wife

32 suami
husband

33 saudara
relatives

34 jumlah
amount

35 ipar laki-laki
brother-in-law

36 ipar perempuan
sister-in-law

37 menantu laki-laki
son-in-law

38 menantu perempuan
daughter-in-law

39 Anda
you/your (formal)

40 kamu
you/your (informal)

41 saya
I/my (formal)

42 aku
I/my (informal)

43 paman
uncle (parent's younger
brother)

44 tanté
aunty (for older
European female)

45 om
uncle (for older
European male)

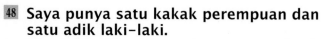

47 Berapa jumlah saudaramu?
How many brothers and sisters
do you have?

**48 Saya punya satu kakak perempuan dan
satu adik laki-laki.**
I have one elder sister and one younger brother.

8 kakek grandfather

9 nenek grandmother

suami dan istri husband and wife

11 saudara laki-laki brother

13

15 saudara perempuan sister

10 pakde uncle (parent's older brother)

12 bapak father

14 ibu mother

16 bibi aunt (parent's younger sister)

17 kakak perempuan older sister

18 kakak laki-laki older brother

19 saya I; me

20 adik perempuan younger sister

21 adik laki-laki younger brother

46 Keluarga kami tinggal di Yogyakarta. Our family lives in Yogyakarta.

23 sepupu cousins

22 kemenakan laki-laki nephew

24 kemenakan perempuan niece

13

3 Di rumah
At home

5 **kunci**
keys

1 **ruang tamu**
living room

2 **tangga**
staircase

3 **lampu**
light

4 **langit-langit**
ceiling

6 **taman**
garden

9 **pintu**
door

13 **guling**
bolster

14 **kursi**
chair

10 **bantal**
cushion

7 **televisi**
television

11 **sofa**
sofa

8 **karpet**
carpet

12 **meja**
table

15 **gambar**
painting

16 **kamar tidur**
bedroom

17 **tirai**
curtain

18 **kipas angin**
fan

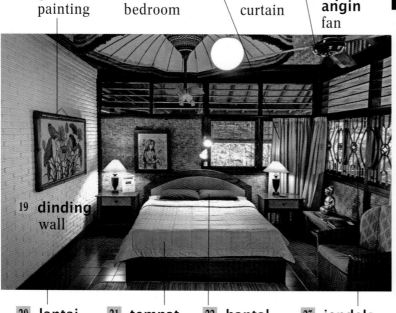

19 **dinding**
wall

20 **lantai**
floor

21 **tempat tidur**
bed

22 **bantal**
pillow

23 **jendela**
window

Additional Vocabulary

51 **kamar**
room

52 **AC** *(Ah-sey)*
airconditioner

53 **saklar lampu**
light switch

54 **soket listrik**
power socket

55 **apartemen**
apartment

56 **lantai/tingkat**
floors/levels

57 **mewah**
luxurious

58 **dijual**
for sale

59 **garasi**
garage

60 **atap**
roof

61 **halaman depan**
frontyard

62 **halaman belakang**
backyard

63 **disewakan**
for rent

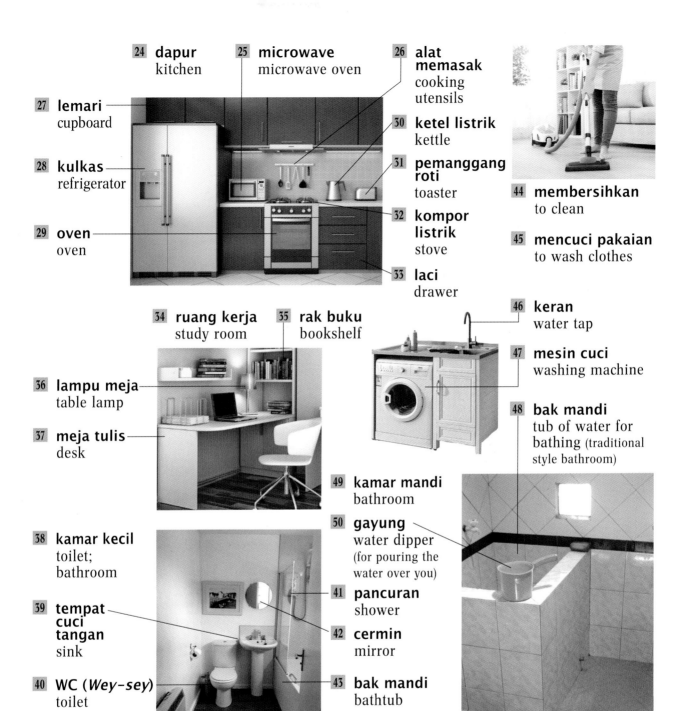

24 **dapur**
kitchen

25 **microwave**
microwave oven

26 **alat memasak**
cooking utensils

27 **lemari**
cupboard

28 **kulkas**
refrigerator

29 **oven**
oven

30 **ketel listrik**
kettle

31 **pemanggang roti**
toaster

32 **kompor listrik**
stove

33 **laci**
drawer

44 **membersihkan**
to clean

45 **mencuci pakaian**
to wash clothes

34 **ruang kerja**
study room

35 **rak buku**
bookshelf

36 **lampu meja**
table lamp

37 **meja tulis**
desk

46 **keran**
water tap

47 **mesin cuci**
washing machine

48 **bak mandi**
tub of water for bathing (traditional style bathroom)

49 **kamar mandi**
bathroom

50 **gayung**
water dipper (for pouring the water over you)

38 **kamar kecil**
toilet; bathroom

39 **tempat cuci tangan**
sink

40 **WC** (*Wey-sey*)
toilet

41 **pancuran**
shower

42 **cermin**
mirror

43 **bak mandi**
bathtub

64 **Ada berapa kamar di rumah ini?**
How many bedrooms does this house have?

65 **Apartemen ini disewakan.**
This apartment is for rent.

66 **Apakah Anda mencari rumah yang dijual di Jakarta?**
Are you looking for a house for sale in Jakarta?

67 **Di mana kamar mandi?**
Where is the bathroom?

4 | Bagian tubuh
Parts of the body

1 rambut
hair

2 kepala
head

3 alis
eyebrow

4 mata
eye

5 telinga
ear

6 hidung
nose

7 leher
neck

8 mulut
mouth

9 pipi
cheek

10 wajah
face

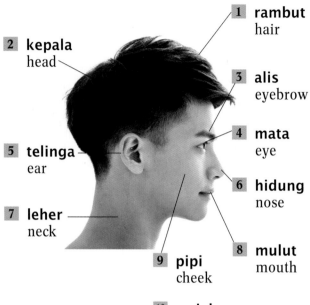

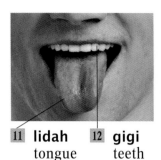

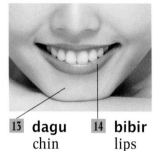

11 lidah
tongue

12 gigi
teeth

13 dagu
chin

14 bibir
lips

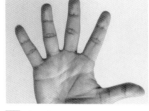

15 jari tangan
fingers

16 jari kaki
toes

58 Ada berapa bagian tubuh yang bisa Anda subutkan?
How many parts of the body can you name?

59 Bagaimana Anda merawat tubuh?
How do you take care of your body?

60 Merokok itu merugikan kesehatan.
Smoking ruins your health.

61 Hati–hati, jangan makan terlalu banyak!
Be careful, don't eat too much!

62 Minum air setiap pagi menyehatkan badan.
Drinking water every morning keeps your body healthy.

63 Dilarang merokok
No smoking

 **17 otak**
brain

 18 paru-paru
lungs

 **19 jantung**
heart

 **20 ginjal**
kidneys

 **21 usus**
intestines

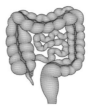 **22 hati**
liver

The word **hati** means liver. It can be used, however, in other contexts which refer to the heart. eg. **baik hati** = kind hearted.

57 Berolahraga setiap hari baik untuk kesehatan.
Exercising every day is good for your health.

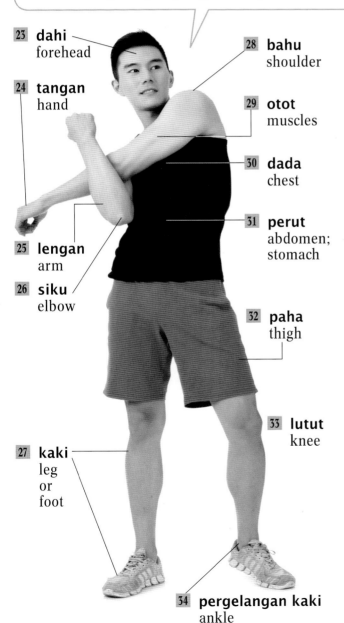

23 dahi
forehead

24 tangan
hand

25 lengan
arm

26 siku
elbow

27 kaki
leg
or
foot

28 bahu
shoulder

29 otot
muscles

30 dada
chest

31 perut
abdomen;
stomach

32 paha
thigh

33 lutut
knee

34 pergelangan kaki
ankle

Additional Vocabulary

35 organ
organs

36 pencernaan
digestion

37 bernapas
to breathe

38 saraf
nerve

39 kerangka
skeleton; frame

40 kulit
skin

41 darah
blood

42 pembuluh darah
blood vessels; vein

43 tulang
bone

44 pembuluh nadi
artery

45 sakit
ill

46 kesakitan
illness

47 sehat
healthy

48 kurang sehat
unhealthy

49 kesehatan
health

50 gizi
nutrition

51 gaya hidup
lifestyle

52 manfaat
benefit

53 amandel
tonsils

54 merawat
to take care of

55 hati-hati
be careful

56 obat
medicine

5 Nomor dan bilangan
Numbers and counting

Cardinal Numbers

 **1** satu
one

 **2** dua
two

 **3** tiga
three

 **4** empat
four

 5 lima
five

 **6** enam
six

 **7** tujuh
seven

 **8** delapan
eight

 **9** sembilan
nine

10 sepuluh
ten

 **12** tiga perempat
three quarters

 **14** sepertiga
one third

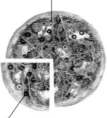 **11** setengah
a half

 **13** seperempat
one quarter

 **15** dua pertiga
two thirds

0 **nol** zero	
11 **sebelas** eleven	
12 **dua belas** twelve	
13 **tiga belas** thirteen	
14 **empat belas** fourteen	
15 **lima belas** fifteen	
16 **enam belas** sixteen	
17 **tujuh belas** seventeen	
18 **delapan belas** eighteen	
19 **sembilan belas** nineteen	
20 **dua puluh** twenty	
21 **dua puluh satu** twenty-one	
22 **dua puluh dua** twenty-two	
23 **dua puluh tiga** twenty-three	
24 **dua puluh empat** twenty-four	
25 **dua puluh lima** twenty-five	
26 **dua puluh enam** twenty-six	
27 **dua puluh tujuh** twenty-seven	
28 **dua puluh delapan** twenty-eight	
29 **dua puluh sembilan** twenty-nine	
30 **tiga puluh** thirty	
40 **empat puluh** forty	
50 **lima puluh** fifty	
60 **enam puluh** sixty	
70 **tujuh puluh** seventy	
80 **delapan puluh** eighty	
90 **sembilan puluh** ninety	
100 **seratus** one hundred	
201 **dua ratus satu** two hundred and one	
1,000 **seribu** one thousand	
10,000 **sepuluh ribu** ten thousand	
100,000 **seratus ribu** one hundred thousand	
1,000,000 **sejuta** one million	
100,000,000 **seratus juta** one hundred million	
1,000,000,000 **milyar** one billion	

18

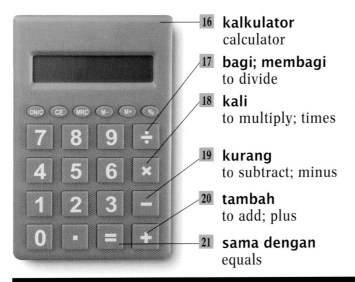

16 kalkulator
calculator

17 bagi; membagi
to divide

18 kali
to multiply; times

19 kurang
to subtract; minus

20 tambah
to add; plus

21 sama dengan
equals

Additional Vocabulary

22 keduanya
both

23 persen
percent (%)

24 pecahan
fraction

25 angka genap
even numbers

26 angka ganjil
odd numbers

27 hitung; menghitung
to count

28 nomor
number

29 digit; angka
digit

30 soal
math (problem)

31 rumus
formula

32 orang
person

Ordinal Numbers
Note: To form an ordinal number, just add **ke-** to the number. In written form, this can be shortened to **ke-10,** etc.

1st **pertama** first
2nd **kedua** second
3rd **ketiga** third
4th **keempat** fourth
5th **kelima** fifth
6th **keenam** sixth
7th **ketujuh** seventh
8th **kedelapan** eighth
9th **kesembilan** ninth
10th **kesepuluh (ke-10)** tenth
11th **kesebelas (ke-11)** eleventh
12th **keduabelas** twelfth
13th **ketigabelas** thirteenth
20th **keduapuluh** twentieth
30th **ketigapuluh** thirtieth
40th **keempatpuluh** fourtieth
50th **kelimapuluh** fiftieth
60th **keenampuluh** sixtieth
70th **ketujuhpuluh** seventieth
80th **kedelapanpuluh** eightieth
90th **kesembilanpuluh** ninetieth
100th **keseratus** hundredth
1,000th **keseribu** thousandth

33 Dua tambah empat sama dengan enam.
Two plus four equals six.

34 Sepuluh dikurangi lima sama dengan lima.
Ten minus five equals five.

35 Lima belas dibagi tiga sama dengan lima.
Fifteen divided by three equals five.

36 Sepuluh kali dua sama dengan dua puluh.
Ten times two equals twenty.

37 Orang muda itu berumur delapan belas dan kakaknya berumur dua puluh lima tahun.
That young person is 18 (years old) and his/her older brother/sister is 25 years old.

6 | Kegiatan sehari-hari
Everyday activities

1 dengar; mendengar
to hear

2 lihat; melihat
to see

5 diri; berdiri
to stand

6 duduk
to sit

3 tawa; tertawa
(coll. ketawa)
to laugh

4 tangis; menangis
(coll. nangis)
to cry

Additional Vocabulary

17 minum
to drink

18 makan
to eat

19 makan siang
to eat lunch

20 makan malam
to have dinner

21 mandi
to take a bath

22 cuci; mencuci
to wash

23 cuci tangan
to wash your hands

24 cuci rambut
to wash your hair

25 cuci piring
to wash the dishes

26 bermain
to play

27 bekerja
to work

28 belajar
to study

29 masak; memasak
to cook

30 waktu luang
free time

31 membersihkan
to clean (something)

32 istirahat
to rest

33 menonton
to watch (a film or TV)

34 menggosok gigi
to brush teeth

35 hari kerja
weekday

36 akhir minggu
weekend

37 hobi
hobby

38 santai; bersantai
to relax

39 laku; melaku(kan)
to do

40 belanja; berbelanja
to shop

41 ikut
to come along;
to follow

42 menikmati
to enjoy

43 suka
to like

44 bersama–sama
together

45 pakai; memakai
to use; wear

46 bantu; membantu
to help

47 **Tidur selama delapan jam baik untuk kesehatan.**
Sleeping for eight hours is good for your health.

8 **bangun**
to wake up

9 **minum kopi**
to drink coffee

7 **tidur**
to sleep

10 **membantu ibu**
to help mum

11 **makan pagi**
to have breakfast

12 **bercakap-cakap**
to chat

13 **bicara**
to talk

14 **mendengarkan (musik)**
to listen to (music)

15 **menulis surat**
write a letter

48 **Sesudah mencuci rambut aku menggosok gigi.**
After washing my hair, I brush my teeth.

16 **sembahyang; berdoa**
to pray

49 **Apa yang Sita lakukan setiap malam sesudah bekerja?**
What do you (Sita) do each night after work?

50 **Kami suka keluar minum kopi.**
We like to go out and have coffee.

51 **Apa Anda lakukan pada akhir minggu?**
What do you do on weekends?

52 **Saya membaca buku atau menonton film.**
I read a book or watch a film.

7 | Warna, bentuk, dan ukuran
Colors, shapes, and sizes

1 **warna**
colors

2 **merah**
red

3 **putih**
white

4 **hitam**
black

5 **kuning**
yellow

6 **biru**
blue

7 **hijau**
green

8 **ungu**
purple

9 **coklat**
brown

10 **abu-abu**
gray

11 **jingga**
orange

12 **merah muda**
pink

13 **emas**
gold

14 **perak**
silver

15 **biru tua**
dark blue

16 **biru muda**
light blue

42 **Apa warna kesukaanmu?**
What is your favorite color?

43 **Warna kesukaanku merah muda.**
My favorite color is pink.

17 **pelangi**
a rainbow

22

 **18 persegi panjang**
a rectangle

 **19 lingkaran**
a circle

 **20 segi delapan**
an octagon

 **21 segi lima**
a pentagon

 **22 kotak**
a square

 **23 hati**
a heart

 **24 oval**
an oval

 25 bintang
a star

 **26 segi tiga**
a triangle

 27 segi enam
a hexagon

28 berlian
a diamond

29 ukuran pakaian
clothing size

30 sedang
M size

31 kecil
S size

32 ekstra kecil
XS size

33 besar
L size

34 ekstra besar
XL size

35 besar
large

36 medium
medium

37 kecil
small

44 Apakah ada ukuran lebih besar?
Do you have a larger size?

45 Apakah ada warna yang lain?
Do you have other colors?

Additional Vocabulary

38 bentuk
shape

39 ukuran
size

40 lebih besar
larger

41 lebih kecil
smaller

8 | **Lawan kata**
Opposites

1 **menerima** ↔ **memberi**
to receive   to give

2 **pendek** ↔ **tinggi**
short   tall

3 **panjang** ↔ **pendek**
long   short

4 **gemuk** ↔ **kurus**
fat   thin

5 **senang** ↔ **sedih**
happy   sad

6 **naik** ↔ **turun**
up   down

7 **baik** ↔ **buruk**
good   bad

8 **lama** ↔ **baru**
old   new

9 **manis** ↔ **pahit**
sweet   bitter

10 **keluar** ↔ **masuk**
exit   enter

11 **kotor** ↔ **bersih**
dirty   clean

12 **dorong** ↔ **tarik**
push   pull

17 **belum** ↔ **sudah**
not yet   already

18 **sulit** ↔ **mudah**
difficult   easy

19 **datang** ↔ **pergi**
to come   to go

13 **tua** ↔ **muda**
old   young

20 **tiba** ↔ **berangkat**
to arrive   to depart

14 **besar** ↔ **kecil**
big   small

21 **berbahaya** ↔ **aman**
dangerous   safe

22 **depan** ↔ **belakang**
front   back

23 **dekat** ↔ **jauh**
near   far

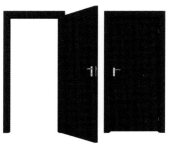

15 **buka** ↔ **tutup**
open   closed

24 **cepat** ↔ **lambat**
fast   slow

25 **berani** ↔ **takut**
brave   afraid

26 **salah** ↔ **benar**
wrong   right

27 **banyak** ↔ **sedikit**
a lot   a little

16 **lebih** ↔ **kurang**
more   less

28 **tinggi** ↔ **rendah**
high   low; lowered

29 **lupa** ↔ **ingat**
to forget   to remember

30 **tebal** ↔ **tipis**
thick   thin

31 **kenyang** ↔ **lapar**
full (with food)   hungry

32 **pinjam** ↔ **kembalikan**
to borrow   to return (something)

33 **masa lalu** ↔ **masa depan**
the past   the future

---

34 **Orang muda ini pendek tetapi orang itu tinggi.**
This young person is short but that person is tall.

35 **Apakah kantor buka atau tutup?**
Is the office open or closed?

36 **Apakah belajar bahasa Indonesia sulit atau mudah?**
Is learning Indonesian difficult or easy?

9 Uang
Money

3 koin
coins

4 seribu rupiah (Rp1.000)
one thousand rupiah coin

6 uang
money

7 mata uang
currency

8 tunai
cash

2 uang kertas
notes (paper money)

5 dua ratus rupiah (Rp200)
two hundred rupiah coin

1 rupiah
rupiah (the official currency of Indonesia)

9 uang dua ribu rupiah
two thousand rupiah note

10 uang lima ribu rupiah
five thousand rupiah note

11 uang sepuluh ribu rupiah
ten thousand rupiah note

12 uang dua puluh ribu rupiah
twenty thousand rupiah note

13 uang lima puluh ribu rupiah
fifty thousand rupiah note

41 Apakah saya dapat membayar tagihan hotel dengan kartu kredit?
May I pay the hotel bill with credit card?

42 Maaf, kami tidak menerima kartu kredit.
Sorry, we don't take credit cards.

43 Silakan membayar dengan uang tunai saja.
Please just pay with cash.

44 Berapakah kurs rupiah hari ini?
What is the rupiah exchange rate today?

14 uang seratus ribu rupiah
one hundred thousand rupiah note

15 uang kembali
change (from a purchase)

16 uang tabungan
savings

17 kartu kredit
credit card

18 cek
check; cheque

19 kurs
exchange rate

20 menarik uang
to withdraw money

Additional Vocabulary

21 harga
price

22 diskon
discount

23 harga pas
fixed price

24 murah
cheap

25 mahal
expensive

26 bunga
interest

27 pajak
tax

28 utang
debt

29 bayar; membayar
to pay

30 tawar; menawar
to bargain; negotiate

31 nomor rekening
account number

32 pinjaman
loan

33 pinjaman bank
a bank loan

34 simpanan bank
bank deposit

35 ATM (ah-teh-em)
ATM machine

36 bon
bill

37 tanda terima
receipt

38 cicilan
installment

39 valuta asing
foreign currency

40 uang kecil
small change

45 Berapa harganya?
How much does this cost?

46 Tiga ratus dua puluh ribu rupiah.
Three hundred and twenty thousand rupiah.

47 Bisa kasih diskon?
Can you give a discount?

48 Tidak, harganya pas.
No, it's a fixed price.

10 | **Berbelanja**
Going shopping

1 **jual; menjual**
to sell

2 **Harganya berapa?**
How much is it?

3 **beli; membeli**
to buy

4 **tas belanja**
shopping bag

5 **belanja; berbelanja**
to shop; go shopping

6 **jam tangan**
watch

7 **pakaian**
clothes

8 **kaos**
T-shirt

9 **kemeja**
men's shirt

10 **baju perempuan**
blouse

11 **kaus kaki**
socks

12 **dasi**
necktie

14 **jin**
jeans

15 **celana**
trousers

13 **rok**
skirt

16 **sepatu**
shoes

17 **topi**
hat

Some useful shopping expressions:

48 **Oleh-oleh bisa beli di mana?**
Where can souvenirs be bought?

49 **Lihat-lihat dulu.**
(I'll) look around first.

50 **Boleh saya coba ini?**
May I try this on?

51 **Di mana kamar pas?**
Where is the fitting room?

52 **Bayar di mana?**
Where do I pay?

53 **Terlalu mahal!**
Too expensive!

54 **Saya mau beli ini.**
I'll buy this one.

55 **Bisa kurang?**
Can you reduce (the price)?

56 **Ya, bisa kurang sedikit.**
Yes, (I) can reduce (the price) a little.

57 **Minta tanda terima.**
Please give me a receipt

58 **Terima kasih, Bu.**
Thank you, Madam.

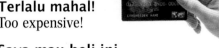

Additional Vocabulary

25 **toko**
shop

26 **toko serba ada**
department store

27 **kasir**
cashier

28 **pengiriman ke rumah**
home delivery

29 **biaya pengiriman**
delivery cost

30 **perbandingan harga**
comparing prices

31 **belanja online**
online shopping

32 **bayar; membayar**
to pay

33 **sama seperti**
the same as

34 **bersama dengan**
together with

35 **mahal**
expensive

36 **lebih mahal**
more expensive

37 **murah**
cheap

38 **lebih murah**
cheaper

39 **obral**
sale

40 **oleh-oleh**
souvenirs

41 **uang kembali**
change

42 **barang**
goods; things

43 **tagihan**
bill; invoice

44 **bebas pajak**
tax free

45 **mau**
to want

46 **pakai; memakai**
to wear; use

47 **minta**
to ask for

18 **kain dan kebaya**
a traditional batik skirt and blouse

19 **jilbab**
hijab (head covering)

20 **ikat pinggang**
belt

21 **syal**
scarf

22 **kaca mata**
glasses; spectacles

23 **kosmetik**
cosmetics

24 **mainan**
toys

11 | **Di kota**
In the city

1 **bandar udara (bandara)**
airport

2 **gedung**
building

3 **jembatan penyeberangan**
pedestrian bridge

4 **jalan**
road; street

5 **jalan raya**
main road

6 **ramai**
busy

7 **ibu kota Jakarta**
the capital city of Jakarta

8 **kemacetan lalu lintas**
traffic jam

9 **pom bensin**
petrol station

10 **bank**
bank

11 **gedung konferensi**
conference center

12 **stasiun kereta api**
train station

13 **museum**
museum

14 **kota Jakarta**
the city of Jakarta

15 **hotel**
hotel

16 **pencakar langit**
skyscraper

17 **gedung apartemen**
apartment building

18 **galeri kesenian**
an art gallery

19 **stadiun**
stadium

20 **kantor pos**
post office

21 **pos polisi**
police post

22 **jalan tol**
expressway

23 **toko swalayan;
pasar swalayan**
supermarket

Additional Vocabulary

24 **toko**
shops

25 **pusat kota**
city center

26 **pusat kawasan
bisnis**
central business
district (CBD)

27 **pinggiran kota**
suburbs

28 **pusat
perbelanjaan**
shopping center

29 **mal**
mall (shopping
center)

30 **bioskop**
cinema

31 **rumah**
house

32 **tetangga**
neighbor

33 **jembatan**
bridge

34 **sudut jalan**
street corner

35 **trotoar**
sidewalk;
pavement

36 **monumen**
monument

37 **lalu lintas**
traffic

38 **populasi**
population

39 **pejalan kaki**
pedestrian

40 **tempat
penyeberangan**
pedestrian crossing

41 **lampu lalu lintas**
traffic lights

42 **kantor polisi**
police station

43 **satu arah**
one-way (street)

44 **dua arah**
two-way (street)

45 **Anda tinggal di kota mana?**
Which city do you live in?

46 **Di mana ada toko buku?**
Where is there a bookshop?

47 **Bandara berapa jauhnya dari sini?**
How far is the airport from here?

48 **Jalan Malioboro adalah jalan
rayanya kota Yogyakarta.**
Malioboro Street is the main street of
Yogyakarta (see photo below).

12 Transportasi
Transport

1 mobil
car

2 ojek
motorcycle taxi

3 taksi
taxi

4 sopir
driver

5 pesawat terbang
airplane

6 sepeda motor
motorbike

7 mobil pengiriman
delivery van

8 dokar
horse cart

9 kereta api
train

10 bajaj
a motorised three wheel vehicle

11 becak
pedicab

12 **bis; bus**
bus

13 **kapal**
ship

14 **perahu**
sailing boat

15 **truk**
truck

Additional Vocabulary

18 **naik**
to go on; to go by__

19 **naik bus**
to take a bus

20 **naik mobil**
to go by car

21 **naik pesawat**
to go by plane

22 **pelan–pelan**
slow (down)

23 **lebih cepat**
faster

24 **pesan; memesan (tiket)**
to book (a ticket)

25 **belok kiri**
turn left

26 **belok kanan**
turn right

27 **terus; lurus**
go straight

28 **jadwal kereta api**
train schedule

29 **loket; tempat penjualan karcis**
ticket office

30 **rute bis**
bus route

31 **panggil taksi**
hail a taxi

32 **penumpang**
passenger

33 **halte bus; tempat perhentian bus**
bus stop

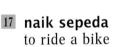

16 **mobil pemadam kebakaran**
fire engine

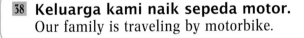

17 **naik sepeda**
to ride a bike

38 **Keluarga kami naik sepeda motor.**
Our family is traveling by motorbike.

34 **Naik apa ke sana?**
How can I get there (By what mode of transport)?

35 **Naik taksi atau naik bis bisa.**
You can go by taxi or bus.

36 **Di mana stasiun kereta api?**
Where is the train station?

37 **Pesan tiket dari internet lebih cepat.**
Booking a ticket from the internet is faster.

13 Mau ke mana?
Where are you going?

1 pergi
to go

47 Mau ke mana?
Where do you want to go?

48 Kami pulang ke rumah, Mas, ke Jalan Solo.
We are returning home, Mas, to Solo Street.

2 pulang
to return home

3 di dalam
inside

5 di luar
outside

4 di depan
at the front

6 di belakang
at the back

Some common phrases used when asking and giving directions:

49 Maaf Pak, saya tersesat. Apakah jalan ini menuju ke pusat kota?
Excuse me, Sir, I'm lost. Does this road go to the city center?

50 Ya, terus saja kalau ingin ke pusat kota.
Yes, just straight ahead if you want to go to the city center.

7 belok ke kiri
turn left

51 Saya mau pergi ke Ubud.
I want to go to Ubud.

52 Di mana Pusat Kesenian?
Where is the Arts Center?

53 Berapa jauh? Dua kilometer.
How far is it? Two kilometers.

54 Permisi, boleh saya tanya? Di mana kantor pariwisata?
Excuse me, may I ask you? Where is the tourist office?

55 Maaf saya tidak tahu.
Sorry, I don't know.

56 Di sebelah kiri/kanan.
It's on the left/right.

57 Di samping pom bensin.
Next to the petrol station.

58 Bisa tolong ditunjukkan?
Can you point it out?

59 Putar balik, kemudian...
Turn around, then...

60 Berjalan melewati jembatan.
Walk over the bridge.

61 Saya tersesat.
I'm lost.

8 lurus
go straight ahead

9 belok ke kanan
turn right

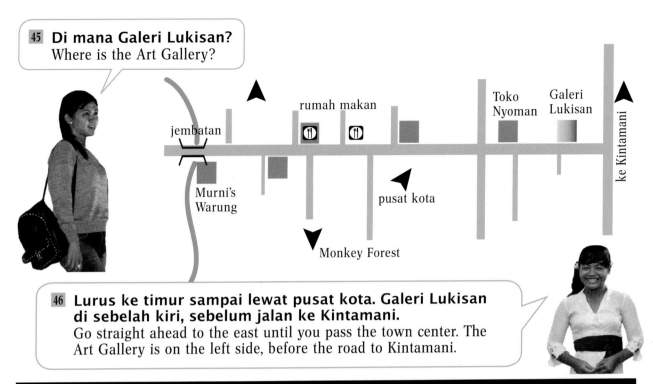

45 **Di mana Galeri Lukisan?**
Where is the Art Gallery?

46 **Lurus ke timur sampai lewat pusat kota. Galeri Lukisan di sebelah kiri, sebelum jalan ke Kintamani.**
Go straight ahead to the east until you pass the town center. The Art Gallery is on the left side, before the road to Kintamani.

Additional Vocabulary

10 **arah**
direction

11 **jarak**
distance

12 **Berapa jaraknya?**
What is the distance?

13 **meter**
meter

14 **dekat/jauh**
near/far

15 **seberang**
opposite; across from

16 **utara**
north

17 **selatan**
south

18 **timur**
east

19 **barat**
west

20 **di samping**
beside

21 **di sini**
here

22 **di sana**
there

23 **cari; mencari**
to look for

24 **lewat; melewati**
to go past or through

25 **berangkat**
to leave

26 **Berapa lama?**
How long?

27 **segera**
soon; immediately

28 **cepat**
quick(ly)

29 **boleh**
may (I)

30 **bantu; membantu**
to help

31 **masuk**
to enter

32 **terus**
to continue (on)

33 **Tunggu sebentar.**
Wait a moment.

34 **jalan**
road (also to go)

35 **berhenti**
to stop

36 **berjalan kaki**
to walk

37 **sampai**
until

38 **tanya; bertanya**
to ask

39 **tempat**
place

40 **ke mana?**
where to?

41 **di mana?**
where?

42 **mau**
to want

43 **ke**
to

44 **dari**
from

14 | Cuaca
The weather

1 payung
umbrella

2 jas hujan
raincoat

3 angin
wind

4 berangin
windy

5 hujan
rain; to rain

Jakarta Selatan
Suhu 32°C
Kelembaban 65-95%

11 kepanasan
overcome by heat

6 cerah
clear (sky)

7 berawan
cloudy day

9 panas
hot

8 pelangi
rainbow

10 lembab
humid

12 halilintar
lightning

13 guntur
thunder

14 badai
storm

15 salju
snow

16 topan
typhoon

38 Cuaca hari ini cerah, tapi besok akan turun hujan.
The weather is fine today, but tomorrow it will rain.

39 Hari ini sangat panas. Suhunya mencapai 38 derajat Celcius.
It is very hot today. The temperature has reached 38 degrees Celcius.

40 **Hati-hati, jalannya banjir!**
Careful, the street is flooded!

41 **Aduh! Basah kuyup!**
Oh no! Drenched!

17 **banjir**
flood

Additional Vocabulary

26 **cuaca**
weather

27 **prakiraan cuaca**
weather forecast

28 **cuaca baik**
good weather

29 **cuaca buruk**
bad weather

30 **angin kencang**
fast/strong wind

31 **derajat**
degrees (temp)

32 **sejuk**
cool

33 **mendung**
overcast

34 **kebanjiran**
overcome by
flood; flooded

35 **basah**
wet

36 **terjebak dalam hujan**
caught in the
rain

37 **kemalaman**
caught out in the
dark

18 **dingin**
cold

19 **kedinginan**
overcome by cold

20 **awan**
cloud(s)

21 **kabut**
fog

22 **hujan badai**
rainstorm

23 **hujan es**
hail

24 **matahari**
sun

25 **bulan**
moon

15 Jam berapa sekarang?
What time is it now?

4 jam enam
6 o'clock

5 jam enam lewat lima menit
five minutes past six

1 jam
hour

2 menit
minute

3 detik
second

6 jam
o'clock;
hour;
clock

9 jam enam lewat lima belas menit
fifteen minutes past six

10 jam setengah tujuh
half past six

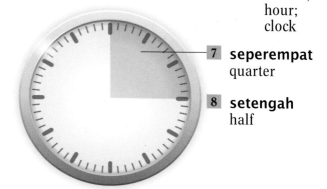

7 seperempat
quarter

8 setengah
half

11 jam tujuh kurang seperempat
a quarter to seven

12 jam tujuh kurang lima menit
five minutes to seven

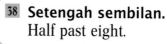

37 Jam berapa sekarang?
What time is it now?

38 Setengah sembilan.
Half past eight.

13 jam beker
alarm clock

14 alat ukur waktu
stopwatch

15 jam tangan pintar
smartwatch

16 jam tangan
wrist watch

39 Maaf, saya terlambat.
Sorry, I'm late.

40 Tidak apa-apa.
It's OK.

41 Jam berapa temanmu datang?
What time will your friend arrive?

42 Saya tidak tahu.
I don't know.

43 Jam berapa pertemuan dimulai?
What time does the meeting start?

44 Jam sembilan pagi.
At 9 o'clock in the morning.

Additional Vocabulary

17 waktu
time

18 pagi
morning

19 malam
night

20 tengah hari
noon

21 sore
late afternoon

22 tengah malam
midnight

23 tepat waktu
punctual

24 awal
early

25 terlambat
late

26 kemudian
later

27 sebelum
before

28 belum
not yet

29 sebentar
a brief moment

30 sudah
already

31 sesudah
after

32 dahulu
in the past

33 sering
frequently

34 sebentar
in a moment

35 pada akhirnya
finally

36 tiba-tiba
suddenly

16 Tahun dan tanggal
Years and dates

> **53** **Saya suka menulis di buku harian.**
> I like to write in a diary.

1 kalender	**2** bulan	**3** tahun	**4** hari	**5** buku harian	**6** tanggal
calendar	month	year	day	diary	date

01 **JANUARI**

SENIN	SELASA	RABU	KAMIS	JUMAT	SABTU	MINGGU
1	2	3	4	5	6	7
8	9	10	11	12	13	14
15	16	17	18	19	20	21
22	23	24	25	26	27	28
29	30	31				

11 hari **Minggu** Sunday
12 hari **Senin** Monday
13 hari **Selasa** Tuesday
14 hari **Rabu** Wednesday
15 hari **Kamis** Thursday
16 hari **Jumat** Friday
17 hari **Sabtu** Saturday

7 kemarin	**8** hari ini	**9** besok
yesterday	today	tomorrow

10 **undangan**
invitation

54 **Hari ini hari Jumat, 27 Januari.**
Today is Friday, January 27.

55 **Kemarin hari Kamis, 26 Januari.**
Yesterday was Thursday, January 26.

56 **Besok hari Sabtu, 28 Januari.**
Tomorrow will be Saturday, January 28.

57 **Hari ulang tahun saya 5 Juli.**
My birthday is on the 5th of July.

Undangan

Hai Teman-Teman datang yaa
ke ulang tahunku
Dewi Mulyani

Hari   hari Sabtu

Tanggal   5 Juli

Jam   6.00 sore

Tempat   Jl. Berlian 17

How to express years, months and dates in Indonesian.

2002 = **tahun dua ribu dua**

2021 = **tahun dua ribu dua puluh satu**

1990 = **tahun sembilan belas sembilan puluh**

2013 = **tahun dua ribu tiga belas**

The 12 months of the year in Indonesian are:

18 **Januari** January

19 **Februari** February

20 **Maret** March

21 **April** April

22 **Mei** May

23 **Juni** June

24 **Juli** July

25 **Agustus** August

26 **September** September

27 **Oktober** October

28 **November** November

29 **Desember** December

Dates are expressed with the date first followed by the month. For example:

February 5 = **5 Februari**

March 31 = **31 Maret**

April 1 = **1 April**

July 4 = **4 Juli**

December 25 = **25 Desember**

58 **Tanggal berapa Anda berangkat?**
What date are you leaving?

59 **Pada tanggal 16 Februari.**
On the 16th of February.

Additional Vocabulary

30 **tahun ini**
this year

31 **tahun lalu**
last year

32 **tahun depan**
next year

33 **tahun sebelumnya**
the year before

34 **tahun berikutnya**
year after next

35 **minggu**
week

36 **minggu lalu**
last week

37 **dua minggu yang lalu**
two weeks ago

38 **minggu depan**
next week

39 **bulan lalu**
last month

40 **bulan depan**
next month

41 **sepuluh tahun**
ten years

42 **bertahun-tahun**
over many years

43 **berumur dua tahun**
2 years (of age)

44 **hari ulang tahun**
birthday; anniversary

45 **tahun kabisat**
leap year

46 **darsawarsa**
decade

47 **abad**
century

48 **milenium**
millennium

49 **selama**
during

50 **libur; liburan**
holiday

51 **tanggal lahir**
birth date

52 **peringatan**
memorial; commemoration

Ke dokter
To the doctor

1 perawat
nurse

2 dokter
doctor

3 pasien
patient

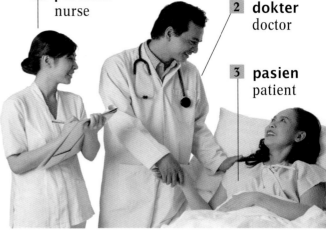

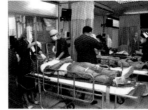

4 rumah sakit
hospital

6 ruang darurat
emergency room

5 ruang tunggu
waiting room

7 minum obat
to take medicine

8 obat
medicine

9 pil
pill

10 uji laboratorium
laboratory test

11 suntik
injection

12 masuk angin
to catch a cold

13 batuk
to cough

14 sakit tenggorokan
sore throat

15 demam
fever

16 jatuh sakit
to fall sick

58 Saya menunggu dokter karena anak saya sudah dua hari sakit.
I am waiting for the doctor because my child has been sick for two days.

17 tekanan darah tinggi
high blood pressure

18 tekanan darah
blood pressure

19 tekanan darah rendah
low blood pressure

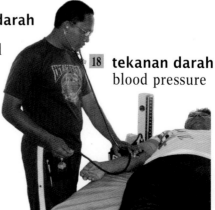

Additional Vocabulary

20 sakit
to be sick; to hurt

21 sakit perut
stomach ache

22 sakit kepala
headache

23 janjian
appointment

24 berjanjian
to make an
appointment

25 ambulans
ambulance

26 dokter gigi
dentist

27 praktek dokter
doctor's practice

**28 telingga, hidung
dan tenggorokan**
ear, nose and throat

29 puskesmas
local health service

30 fisioterapy
physiotherapy

31 kecelakaan
accident

32 resep
prescription

33 apotek
pharmacy

34 antiseptik
antiseptic

35 luka
wound; cut

36 patah
broken

37 keadaan darurat
emergency

38 lelah
tired; worn out

39 pusing
dizzy

40 merasa lemas
to feel faint

41 menderita
to suffer

**42 menderita dari
Malaria**
to suffer from
Malaria

43 beberapa kali
several times

44 takaran
dosage

45 dua kali sehari
twice a day

46 cepat sembuh
get well quickly

47 khawatir
to worry

48 jangan khawatir
don't worry

49 spesialis
specialist

50 penting
important

51 surat dokter
doctor's certificate

**52 pertolongan
pertama**
first aid

53 obat tradisional
traditional medicine

54 pijat
massage

55 antibiotik
antibiotics

56 jamu
herbal remedy

57 penjual jamu
herbal drinks seller

59 Bapak sakit apa?
What is wrong with you, Sir?

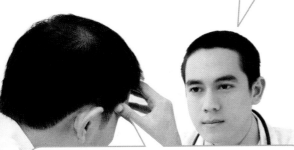

**60 Saya merasa demam dan sakit
tenggorokan.**
I have a fever and a sore throat.

61 Aku merasa kurang sehat.
I am not feeling well.

62 Saya ingin ke dokter.
I would like to see a doctor.

63 Sudah berapa lama sakit?
How long have you been sick?

64 Anda menderita dehidrasi.
You are suffering from dehydration.

**65 Minum obat ini dua kali sehari
sesudah makan.**
Take this medicine twice a day after
eating.

43

18 Agama dan kepercayaan
Religion and beliefs

1 mesjid
mosque

2 bulan puasa
the fasting month

3 menganut
to follow (a religion)

4 salat
the ritual of praying
five times a day

5 agama Islam
the Islamic religion

6 bersembahyang; berdoa
to pray

7 orang Islam
an Islamic person

8 Ramadan
fasting month

9 Lebaran
end of the fasting month

10 ketupat
rice cakes
boiled in
woven coconut
leaves

11 opor ayam
a chicken curry often
eaten at Lebaran

Selamat Hari Raya
Idul Fitri

Mohon maaf lahir bathin

12 Hari Raya Idul Fitri
a celebration at the end of
Ramadan

13 Mohon maaf lahir batin
Please forgive my sins

14 Borobudur
an ancient Buddhist
temple in Central Java

15 agama
religion

16 agama Budha
Buddhism

17 klenteng
a Chinese temple

18 Hari Raya Waisak
Buddha's birthday

19 agama Hindu
Hindu religion

20 Hari Galungan
the day when the Balinese
ancestral spirits visit earth

21 sesajen
offering(s)

22 pura
Hindu-Bali
temple

23 bersembahyang di pura
praying at the temple

24 menjunjung sesajen
to carry offerings on the
head (to the temple)

25 Hari Raya Nyepi
Balinese New Year (a day
of silence)

26 kremasi
cremation
(in Balinese: **ngaben**)

27 gamelan beleganjur
processional gamelan
musicians

28 agama Katolik
Catholic religion

29 agama Kristen
Protestant religion

30 gereja
church

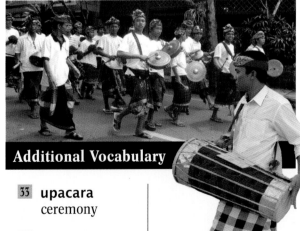

Additional Vocabulary

31 Paskah
Easter

32 Hari Natal
Christmas

33 upacara
ceremony

34 kepercayaan
belief(s)

35 tradisi
tradition

36 percaya
to believe

37 Tuhan
God

38 qur'an
the koran

39 beragama
to have a religion

19 | **Perayaan** Celebrations

1 **bendera Indonesia**
the Indonesian flag

2 **Hari Tahun Baru**
New Year's Day

3 **Hari Raya Nyepi**
Balinese New Year
(a day of silence)

4 **Selamat Tahun Baru!**
Happy New Year!

32 **Selamat hari ulang tahun ke-enam.**
Happy 6th birthday!

5 **memberi hadiah**
to give a gift

7 **ulang tahun**
birthday; anniversary

6 **tumpeng**
a yellow rice cone for celebrations

8 **kue ulang tahun**
a birthday cake

9 **Sekaten**
a week-long Javanese ceremony celebrating the birth of the prophet Muhammad

10 **Hari Ibu**
Mothers Day
(commemoration of first Indonesian Women's Congress held on 22 December 1928)

12 **Hari Kartini**
Kartini Day
(celebrating the woman who started the first Indonesian school for girls)

11 **Hari Ayah**
Fathers Day
(Not an official day in Indonesia)

13 Hari Kasih Sayang
Valentine's Day

33 Saya suka merayakan hari Valentine di tempat istimewa.
I like to celebrate Valentine's day in a special place.

34 Selamat Hari Natal.
Merry Christmas.

14 pohon Natal
Christmas tree

16 coklat
chocolate

17 mawar merah
red rose

15 hadiah
gift; present

18 kembang api
fireworks

19 Tahun Baru Imlek
Chinese New Year

20 Hari Kemerdekaan
Independence Day

21 Hari Kesaktian Pancasila (Tanggal 1 Juni)
Celebrating the five governing principles of Indonesia (June 1)

22 perkawinan Jawa
a Javanese wedding

23 perkawinan Islam di Jawa
an Islamic wedding in Java

Additional Vocabulary

24 perayaan
celebration

25 merayakan
to celebrate

26 pesta ulang tahun
birthday party

27 pengantin laki-laki
groom

28 pengantin wanita
bride

29 diundang
to be invited

30 pernikahan
marriage

31 kelahiran
birth

20 | Di kelas
In class

1 **papan tulis putih**
whiteboard

2 **papan tulis**
writing board

3 **perpustakaan**
library

4 **ruang kelas**
classroom

5 **mengajar** **6** **guru** **7** **belajar**
to teach   teacher   to learn; study

9 **mesin fotokopi**
photocopier

10 **angkat tangan**
to raise your hand

11 **memfotokopi**
to photocopy

12 **dosen**
lecturer;
professor

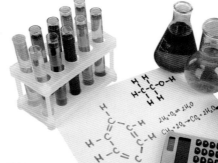

8 **ilmu kimia**
chemistry

13 **kalkulator**
calculator

14 **teman sekelas**
classmates

15 **ruang kuliah**
lecture hall

16 **siswa**
student

54 **Kamu butuh bantuan mengerjakan tugas?**
Do you need help to work out the task?

Additional Vocabulary

17 **sekolah**
school

18 **bersekolah**
to attend school

19 **taman kanak-kanak**
kindergarten

20 **sekolah dasar (SD)**
primary school

21 **sekolah menengah pertama (SMP)**
Junior high school

22 **sekolah menengah atas (SMA)**
Senior high school

23 **universitas**
university

24 **mata pelajaran**
school subject

25 **kuliah**
class at university

26 **mata kuliah**
subject

27 **kepala sekolah**
school principal

28 **nilai**
grades

29 **pandai**
smart

30 **buku tulis**
workbook

31 **buku pelajaran**
textbook

32 **sekolah swasta**
private school

33 **sekolah negeri**
public school

34 **berkuliah**
to attend college or university

35 **jurusan**
major; department

36 **bidang**
field of study

37 **ikut; mengikuti**
to follow; join in

38 **harus**
must

39 **kelas malam**
night class

40 **gelar**
degree

41 **gelar ilmu pengetahuan**
science degree

42 **gelar Master**
Masters degree

43 **lulus**
to finish school

44 **hari wisuda**
graduation day

45 **tamat**
to graduate

46 **bangga**
proud

47 **Doktor Filsafat**
Ph.D

55 **Keluarga kami merasa bangga ketika anak laki-laki kami diwisuda.**
Our family felt proud when our son graduated.

48 **Anda kuliah di mana?**
Where are you studying (university)?

49 **Jam berapa ke kampus?**
What time do you go to campus?

50 **Saya mengikuti kursus bahasa Indonesia yang intensif.**
I am taking an intensive Indonesian language course.

51 **Anda pelajari bidang apa?**
What field are you studying?

52 **Saya jurusan matematika di universitas Surabaya.**
I'm majoring in maths at Surabaya university.

53 **Anda sangat pandai!**
You are very smart!

21 Anda belajar apa?
What are you studying?

1 belajar
to learn; to study

2 baca;
membaca
to read

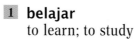

3 ujian
exam

4 matematika
mathematics

5 bahasa asing
foreign languages

6 kosa kata
vocabulary

7 jawab; menjawab
to answer

9 kamus
dictionary

8 buku
book

10 kabar; berita
the news

11 surat kabar
newspaper

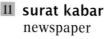

12 majalah
magazine

13 buku tulis
notebook

14 pena
pen

15 stabilo
highlighter

16 pensil
pencil

17 penghapus
eraser

19 rautan pensil
pencil sharpener

21 gunting
scissors

18 spidol
marker pen

20 penggaris
ruler

Additional Vocabulary

22 kelas
grade; class

23 mengerti
to understand

24 berlatih
to practice

25 meninjau
to review

26 masalah
problem; issue

27 pekerjaan rumah
homework

28 kata
word

29 cerita
story

30 ilmu seni dan budaya
arts and culture

31 tugas
assignment; task

32 teknologi informasi
information technology

33 sastra
literature

34 sejarah
history

35 ilmu pengetahuan
science

36 ekonomi
economics

37 ilmu fisika
physics

38 ilmu kimia
chemistry

39 biologi
biology

40 geografi
geography

41 sosiologi
sociology

42 ilmu jasmani
physical education

43 musik
music

44 maksud
purpose

45 komunikasi
communications

46 rajin
diligent

47 pertukaran siswa
student exchange

48 pendidikan
education

49 ambil; mengambil
to take

50 tulis; menulis
to write

51 kedokteran
medicine

52 beasiswa
scholarship

53 pertanyaan
question

54 Mata pelajaran kesukaan Anda apa?
What is your favorite subject?

55 Saya suka belajar bahasa Inggris.
I like studying English.

22 | **Komputer dan Internet**
Computers and the Internet

1 layar
screen

2 komputer
computer

3 tablet
tablet

75 **Saya senang mengobrol dengan teman menggunakan Whatsapp.**
I like to chat with my friends using Whatsapp.

4 **media sosial**
social media

5 **keyboard**
keyboard

6 **laptop**
laptop

8 gim video
video game

7 tetikus
computer mouse

9 bantalan mouse
mousepad

10 USB
USB drive

11 CD/DVD
CD/DVD

12 surel;
email
email

13 cara
way; method

14 memindai
to scan

Additional Vocabulary

15 port
port

16 buat; membuat
to create

17 sendiri
by one's self

18 beranda
homepage

19 berita
news

20 e-majalah
e-magazine

21 daring/luring
online/offline

22 peramban
browser

23 wifi
wifi

24 pranala
links

25 profil
profile

26 album foto
photo album

27 kliping
press clippings

Beranda | Profil | Berita | Album Foto | Kliping | E-Majalah

Additional Vocabulary

28 **akses Internet**
Internet access

29 **sistem operasi**
operating system

30 **terhubung**
to go online

31 **masuk**
to sign in

32 **nama pengguna**
user name

33 **kata sandi**
password

34 **klik**
to click

35 **hapus;
menghapus**
to delete

36 **salin/tempel**
copy/paste

37 **gambar**
image

38 **edit; mengedit**
to edit

39 **situs web**
website

40 **halaman web**
web page

41 **telusuri;
menelusuri**
to search for

42 **mencari**
online search

43 **unggah**
to upload

44 **mengunduh**
to download

45 **mengunduh
data**
to download data

46 **simpan;
menyimpan**
to save

47 **tersimpan**
saved

48 **ketik; mengetik**
to type

49 **kirim; mengirim**
to send

50 **pakai; memakai**
to use

51 **suka**
to like

52 **perangkat lunak**
software

53 **aplikasi**
application

54 **dokumen**
file

55 **jaringan**
network

56 **sambungan**
connection

57 **peladen**
server

58 **desain**
design

59 **interaktif**
interactive

60 **ruang obrolan**
chat room

61 **ngobrol; mengobrol**
to chat

62 **alamat URL**
URL address

63 **kabel**
cable

64 **menurut**
according to

65 **karena; sebab**
because

66 **termasuk**
including

67 **hak cipta**
copyright

68 **warnet (warung
Internet)**
Internet cafe

69 **kotak surat**
mailbox

70 **pengaturan; setelan**
settings

74 **Hobi saya bermain gim daring.**
My hobby is playing online games.

71 **Ayo ngobrol online!**
C'mon, let's chat online!

72 **Aplikasi apa yang Anda pakai? Saya pakai Whatsapp.**
What app do you use? I use Whatsapp.

73 **Saya akan kirim PDF itu lewat email.**
I will send you the PDF by email.

23 Menggunakan ponsel pintar
Using a smartphone

1 **ponsel pintar; smartphone**
smartphone

2 **selfie**
selfie

3 **belanja online**
online shopping

4 **warnet**
internet cafe

5 **ponsel Android**
Android phones

6 **ponsel iPhone**
iPhone

7 **Twitter**
Twitter

8 **Whatsapp**
Whatsapp

9 **telepon genggam; HP**
mobile phone; handphone

10 **melakukan panggilan telepon**
to make a phone call

11 **menerima panggilan telepon**
to receive a phone call

Additional Vocabulary

14 **nomor telepon**
telephone number

15 **proyek**
project

16 **pengisi daya telepon**
phone charger

17 **kartu telepon**
phone card

18 **kartu prabayar**
prepaid phone card

19 **kartu SIM**
SIM card

20 **SMS; pesan teks**
text message

21 **kirim teks**
to text; send a text

22 **kode negara**
country code

23 **kode daerah**
area code

34 Saya sangat senang menerima pesan teks ini dari Dewi.
I am really pleased to receive this text from Dewi.

Some common telephone phrases:

24 Halo. Ini Jono.
Hello. This is Jono.

35 Aplikasi chat yang mana lebih populer di Indonesia?
Which chat application is more popular in Indonesia?

25 Boleh saya bicara dengan...
May I speak to....

26 Tolong minta dia untuk membalas panggilan saya.
Please ask him/her to return my call.

27 Kapan dia bebas bicara di telepon?
When is he/she free to talk on the phone?

36 WhatsApp sangat popular di Indonesia.
WhatsApp is very popular in Indonesia.

28 Tolong bicara lebih keras sedikit?
Could you speak up a bit?

29 Maaf, Anda salah sambung.
Sorry, you dialed the wrong number.

12 teman online
online friends

30 Tunggu sebentar.
Please wait a moment.

31 Silahkan tinggalkan pesan.
Please leave a message.

32 Siapa yang memanggil?
Who's calling, please?

33 Tolong bicara pelan-pelan.
Please speak a little slower.

13 wefie
wefie

37 iPad bermanfaat untuk mengerjakan tugas sekolah.
The iPad is useful for doing school tasks.

24 | Pekerjaan
Work

1 pengacara
lawyer

2 hakim
judge

3 guru
teacher

4 tukang listrik
electrician

5 insinyur
engineer

6 tukang jahit; penjahit
tailor

7 polisi
policeman

8 akuntan
accountant

9 apoteker
pharmacist

10 penata rambut
hairdresser

11 petani
farmer

12 pelukis
painter

13 pemusik
musician

14 manajer
manager

15 sekretaris
secretary

16 koki; juru masak
chef

17 juru potret
photographer

18 pilot; penerbang
pilot

19 dokter
doctor

20 tukang kebun
gardener

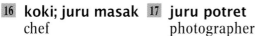

47 Saya belajar di universitas untuk menjadi arsitek.
I studied at university to become an architect.

21 arsitek
architect

48 Anda bekerja di mana?
Where do you work?

49 Saya bekerja sebagai perawat di rumah sakit.
I work as a nurse in a hospital.

50 Saya ingin belajar ilmu kedokteran untuk menjadi dokter di desa.
I want to study medicine in order to become a doctor in a village.

51 Saya masuk kantor pada jam sembilan kurang seperempat pagi.
I go to the office at 8.45 in the morning.

Additional Vocabulary

22 perusahaan
company

23 pengusaha
entrepreneur

24 bisnis
business

25 bekerja
to work

26 pekerjaan
work; job

27 majikan
employer

28 karyawan
employee

29 pengelolaan
management

30 magang
apprentice

31 kerja shift
shift work

32 upah
wage

33 lamaran
job application

34 amar; melamar
to apply

35 cara
method

36 kesempatan
opportunity

37 posisi
position

38 kantor
office

39 dokter hewan
vet

40 dokter gigi
dentist

41 tukang ledeng
plumber

42 tukang kayu
carpenter

43 penterjemah
translator

44 perawat
nurse

45 gaji
salary

46 menjadi
to become

25 Kesenian
The arts

1 **penari**
dancer

2 **tari; menari**
to dance

3 **gitar**
guitar

5 **nyanyi; bernyanyi**
to sing

4 **bermain gitar**
to play the guitar

6 **tari Barong**
Barong dance

42 **Sudah berapa lama bermain gamelan?**
How long have you been playing gamelan?

43 **Sudah sepuluh tahun.**
For ten years.

44 **Tarian ini dari berbagai suku bangsa.**
These dances are from various ethnic groups.

7 **gender**
gender

8 **rebab**
a two stringed bowed instrument

10 **saron**
saron

9 **Gamelan Jawa**
Central Javanese gamelan

11 **kempul**
kempul

13 **gong**
gong

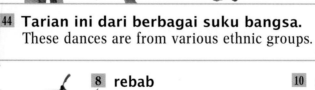

15 **kenong**
kenong

12 **kendang**
drums

14 **bonang**
bonang

16 lukis; melukis
to paint

17 seni
art

18 seniman
artist

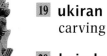

19 ukiran
carving

20 kain batik
batik fabric

21 pewarna
dye

22 lilin
wax

23 canting
a tool for drawing on
fabric with hot wax to
make batik

24 biola
violin

45 Kamu suka musik apa?
What music do you like?

25 Band rock
Rock band

26 keyboard
keyboard

46 Saya mau menjadi
penyanyi terkenal.
I want to become a
famous singer.

27 bermain piano
to play the piano

28 angklung
angklung

29 kecapi dan suling
a plucked zither and a
bamboo flute (from West Java)

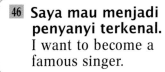

Additional Vocabulary

32 penyanyi
singer

33 terkenal
famous

34 orkes
orchestra

35 menikmati
to enjoy

36 para penonton
audience

37 musik pop
pop music

38 sandiwara
a play

39 pameran
exhibition

40 pertunjukan
performance

41 main; bermain
to play

30 dalang
a puppeteer

31 wayang kulit
shadow puppet

26 Lingkungan alam kita
Our natural environment

1 alam
nature

2 lingkungan
environment; surroundings

5 musim
season

6 musim hujan
rainy season

7 musim kemarau
dry season

3 musim semi
spring

4 musim panas
summer

8 musim gugur
autumn; fall

9 musim dingin
winter

> **52 Hanya ada dua musim di Indonesia, musim hujan dan musim kemarau.**
> There are only two seasons in Indonesia, the rainy season and the dry season.

10 kemboja
frangipani

11 melati
jasmine

12 anggrek
orchid

13 bunga
flower

14 teratai
lotus

15 daun
leaf

16 laut
sea

17 danau
lake

18 sungai
river

19 hutan
forest; jungle

20 pemandangan
view

25 gunung
mountain

26 lembah
valley

21 pohon
tree

27 awan
cloud

22 palem
palm

28 pagi-pagi
early morning

23 kelapa
coconut

29 sepi
quiet

24 taman
park

30 rumput
grass

31 pasir putih
white sand

33 pasir hitam
black sand

35 tanam; menanam
to plant

37 panen; memanen
to harvest

32 pantai
beach

34 ombak
waves

36 sawah
rice fields

38 padi
rice plant

Additional Vocabulary

41 air terjun
waterfall

44 letus; meletus
to erupt

47 margasatwa
wildlife

42 abu
ash

45 tumbuhan
flora; plants

48 gempa bumi
earthquake

43 kawah
crater

46 cagar alam
wildlife sanctuary

49 tsunami
tsunami

39 letusan
eruption

40 gunung api
volcano

50 Ada berapa musim di negara Anda?
How many seasons are there in your country?

51 Musim hujan di Indonesia dari bulan Desember sampai bulan Maret.
The rainy season in Indonesia is from December until March.

27 | Melestarikan lingkungan hidup
Preserving the environment

1 udara
air

2 air
water

3 tanah
earth

4 tumbuhan dan hewan
flora and fauna

5 menanam pohon
to plant trees

6 lestarikan; melestarikan
to preserve

7 lindungi; melindungi
to protect

8 polusi
pollution

9 sampah
rubbish

10 buang; membuang
to throw away

11 tempat
place

Buang Sampah Pada Tempatnya **MERUPAKAN** Budaya Masyarakat **YOGYAKARTA**

aku sudah memulai

diet kantong plastik

kamu?

www.dietkantongplastik.info

www.dietkantongplastik.info

Selamatkan Penyu Dari Kepunahan

12 merupakan
to form; constitute

13 masyarakat
community

14 mulai; memulai
to begin

15 kantong plastik
plastic bag

16 selamat
safe

17 selamatkan
to save

18 punah; kepunahan
extinct; extinction

19 selama
during

53 Kelompok Diet Kantong Plastik menginginkan negara yang bebas dari kantong plastik.
The group Plastic Bag Diet would like a country free of plastic bags.

54 Kita harus melestarikan lingkungan alam di mana pun kita berada.
We must protect our natural environment wherever we are.

20 tenaga angin
wind power

21 tenaga solar
solar energy

22 mobil listrik
electric car

23 daur ulang
recycling

24 tenaga bersih
clean energy

25 kualitas udara
air quality

26 bersih
clean

27 kotor
dirty

28 energi terbarukan
renewable energy

29 tercemar
polluted

30 mencemari
to contaminate

31 pelihara; memelihara
to take care of

32 sembarangan
just anywhere

33 jangan
don't

34 berubah
to change

35 dunia
world

36 oleh karena
because of

37 mendaur ulang
to recycle

38 rusak; merusak
to ruin; destroy

39 dampak
impact

40 akan tetapi
however

41 tentu saja
of course

42 kalau; jikalau
if

43 walaupun
although

44 akibat
result

45 pelestarian lingkungan
environmental conservation

46 kurang; mengurangi
to reduce

47 perubahan iklim
climate change

48 pemanasan global
global warming

49 tujuan
aim; purpose

50 setuju
agree

51 taman nasional
national park

52 pusat rehabilitasi orang utan
orangutan rehabilitation center

55 Jangan membuang sampah sembarangan.
Don't throw rubbish just anywhere.

56 Lebih baik jangan pakai plastik.
It's better not to use plastic.

57 Hari Lingkungan Hidup Sedunia.
World Environment Day.

58 Apakah Anda mendaur ulang?
Do you recycle?

59 Saya mendaur ulang kaca, kertas dan plastik.
I recycle glass, paper and plastic.

63

28 | **Dunia binatang**
The animal world

3 badak
rhinoceros

2 harimau
tiger

1 orang utan
orangutan

4 kakatua
cockatoo

5 cendrawasih
bird of paradise

44 Monyet lebih kecil daripada orang utan.
Monkeys are smaller than orangutans.

45 Komodo adalah kadal monitor terbesar di dunia.
The Komodo dragon is the largest monitor lizard in the world.

46 Ada banyak jenis burung di Indonesia.
There are many species of birds in Indonesia.

6 komodo
komodo dragon

7 kadal monitor
monitor lizard

11 jerapah
giraffe

8 kebun binatang
zoo

9 zebra
zebra

10 penyu
turtle

12 monyet
monkey

13 gajah
elephant

14 buaya
crocodile

15 kerbau
water buffalo

Additional Vocabulary

31 habitat alami
natural habitat

32 lucu
funny; cute

33 buas
fierce

34 jaga; menjaga
to protect; guard

35 jenis
species

36 mirip
to resemble

37 cicak
gecko (house lizard)

38 kodok
frog

39 bebek
duck

40 babi
pig

41 beruang
bear

42 singa
lion

43 lumba-lumba
dolphin

16 kambing
goat

17 domba
sheep

18 sapi
cow

19 kuda
horse

20 ular
snake

21 merak
peacock

22 ayam
chicken

23 burung
bird

24 anjing
dog

25 kucing
cat

26 nyamuk
mosquito

27 capung
dragonfly

28 lebah
bee

29 kupu-kupu
butterfly

30 ikan
fish

65

29 | Gaya hidup yang sehat
A healthy lifestyle

2 raket
racket

3 tenis meja
table tennis

1 bulutangkis
badminton

4 bermain futbal
to play soccer

5 rugbi
rugby

6 bola basket
basketball

7 bermain bola basket
to play basketball

8 baseball
baseball

9 berski
skiing

10 renang; berenang
to swim

11 tenis
tennis

12 olahraga
sport

13 sepeda
bicycle

14 bersepeda
to cycle

15 lari; berlari
to run

16 jogging
to jog

17 golf
golf

18 **pencak silat**
Indonesian self defence

19 **latih; berlatih**
to practice

20 **latihan**
practice (noun)

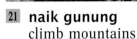

21 **naik gunung**
climb mountains

22 **bola voli**
volleyball

23 **meditasi**
meditation

24 **berselancar**
to surf; surfing

Additional Vocabulary

25 **sedang**
to be in the process of

26 **sedangkan**
whereas

27 **berjalan-jalan**
to go walking; take a stroll

28 **bola**
ball

29 **sehat**
healthy

30 **kesehatan**
health

31 **gaya hidup**
lifestyle

32 **badan**
body

33 **gerak badan**
to work out

34 **menghilangkan**
to eliminate; to lose

35 **menyenangkan**
enjoyable

36 **bersantai**
to relax

37 **hobi**
hobby

38 **bersepatu roda**
to roller skate

---

39 **Apakah Ben suka berolahraga?**
Do you (Ben) like playing sport?

40 **Saya senang jogging sedangkan adik saya senang bermain bola basket.**
I like to jog whereas my younger brother likes to play basketball.

41 **Ada beberapa cara yang menghilangkan stres, misalnya yoga, meditasi atau berpartisipasi dalam kegiatan favorit Anda.**
There are several ways to eliminate stress, for example yoga, meditation or taking part in your favorite activity.

30 Berpergian di Indonesia
Traveling in Indonesia

1 **koper**
suitcase

2 **pakaian**
clothes

3 **sikat rambut**
hairbrush

4 **pakaian renang**
swim suit

5 **tabir surya**
sunscreen

6 **topi**
hat

7 **dompet**
wallet

8 **pelantang**
headphones

9 **ponsel**
mobile phone

10 **kacamata hitam**
sunglasses

11 **kamera**
camera

12 **turis**
tourist

13 **resor**
resort

14 **peta**
map

15 **air terjun**
waterfall

16 **suka**
to like

17 **hotel**
hotel

45 **Air terjun Tumpak Sewu di Jawa Timur adalah air terjun yang paling indah di Indonesia.**
Tumpak Sewu waterfall in East Java is the most beautiful waterfall in Indonesia.

46 **Candi Borobudur adalah objek wisata terkenal di Jawa Tenggah.**
Borobudur temple is a famous tourist attraction in Central Java.

43 **Wisatawan suka berkunjung ke Gunung Bromo.**
Tourists like to visit Mt. Bromo.

18 **objek wisata**
tourist attraction

19 **candi**
ancient temple

20 **kolam renang**
swimming pool

21 **kunjung; berkunjung**
to visit

22 **Danau Toba**
Lake Toba (in Sumatra)

23 **pura**
Balinese Hindu Temple

24 **toko suvenir**
souvenir shop

25 **oleh-oleh**
souvenirs

Additional Vocabulary

27 **naik pesawat**
to go by plane

28 **kantor tiket**
ticket office

29 **pesan; memesan**
to book

30 **kantor pariwisata**
tourist office

31 **matahari terbit**
sunrise

32 **matahari terbenam**
sunset

33 **tunggu; menunggu**
to wait

34 **karcis**
ticket

35 **pantai**
beach

36 **berlibur**
to go on holiday

37 **libur; liburan**
holiday

38 **pemandu**
guide

39 **pemimpin tur**
tour leader

40 **losmen**
small hotel

41 **wisatawan**
tourist

42 **setasiun**
station

44 **Ayo menonton pertunjukan tarian tradisional di Bali!**
Come and watch a traditional dance performance in Bali!

26 **pertunjukan**
performance

47 **Emma akan ke mana waktu liburan?**
Where will you (Emma) go on vacation?

48 **Saya akan berlibur ke Bali.**
I am going on holiday to Bali.

49 **Saya suka pergi ke pantai untuk bermain ombak.**
I like to go to the beach to play in the surf.

50 **Berapa harga paket wisata ke Danau Toba?**
How much is the tourist package to Lake Toba?

31 Berkeliling dunia
Around the world

3 **keliling; berkeliling**
to go around

4 **dunia**
the world

1 **paspor**
passport

2 **visa**
visa

5 **Asia Tenggara**
Southeast Asia

6 **India**
India

10 **Cina**
China

7 **Myanmar**
Myanmar

8 **Thailand**
Thailand

11 **Vietnam**
Vietnam

12 **Laos**
Laos

22 **Filipina**
Philippines

9 **Kamboja**
Cambodia

13 **Malaysia**
Malaysia

14 **bahasa Melayu**
Malay language

21 **Brunei**
Brunei

15 **Singapura**
Singapore

Sumatera

Kalimantan

Sulawesi

Maluku

Papua

16 **bahasa Inggris**
English language

Jawa

Bali *Sumbawa* *Flores*

Lombok *Komodo* *Sumba* *Timor*

17 **bahasa Indonesia**
Indonesian language

18 **bahasa Jawa**
Javanese language

20 **Timor Timur**
East Timor
(Timor Leste)

19 **bahasa Bali**
Balinese language

23 **naik pesawat**
to go by plane

24 **naik kereta api**
to go by train

25 **naik kapal**
to go by ship

26 **naik bus; bis**
to go by bus

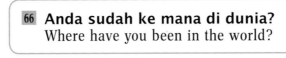

66 **Anda sudah ke mana di dunia?**
Where have you been in the world?

67 **Saya sudah ke Prancis dan Jerman di Eropa, tetapi belum ke negara yang lain.**
I have been to France and Germany in Europe but not yet to other countries.

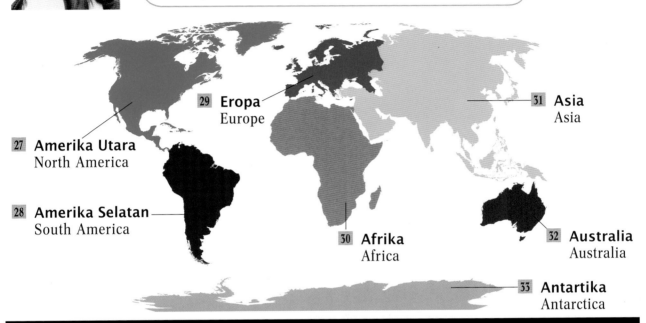

29 **Eropa**
Europe

31 **Asia**
Asia

27 **Amerika Utara**
North America

28 **Amerika Selatan**
South America

30 **Afrika**
Africa

32 **Australia**
Australia

33 **Antartika**
Antarctica

Additional Vocabulary

34 **Kanada**
Canada

35 **Denmark**
Denmark

36 **Finlandia**
Finland

37 **Prancis**
France

38 **Jerman**
Germany

39 **Inggris**
Great Britain

40 **Irlandia**
Ireland

41 **Italia**
Italy

42 **Jepang**
Japan

43 **Korea**
Korea

44 **Meksiko**
Mexico

45 **Belanda**
Netherlands

46 **Selandia Baru**
New Zealand

47 **Norwegia**
Norway

48 **Rusia**
Russia

49 **Swedia**
Sweden

50 **Swiss**
Switzerland

51 **Amerika Serikat**
United States

52 **Samudra Pasifik**
Pacific Ocean

53 **Samudra Hindia**
Indian Ocean

54 **ibu kota**
capital city

55 **perjalanan**
a trip

56 **bea cukai**
customs

57 **vaksinasi**
vaccination

58 **memesan hotel**
to book a hotel

59 **koneksi internet gratis**
free internet connection

60 **memesan secara daring**
to book online

61 **reservasi**
reservation

62 **tamu**
guest

63 **tolong bantu**
please help

64 **tetapi**
but

65 **bahasa**
language

71

32 | Anda berasal dari mana?
Where do you come from?

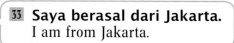

33 **Saya berasal dari Jakarta.**
I am from Jakarta.

34 **Saya berasal dari kota Surabaya.**
I come from the town of Surabaya.

35 **Saya lahir di Yunani dan berbahasa Yunani.**
I was born in Greece and speak Greek.

1 **asal; berasal**
to originate;
come from

36 **Bisa bicara bahasa Indonesia?**
Can you speak Indonesian?

2 **tanah air**
homeland

3 **bisa**
can (to be able)

37 **Saya bisa bicara bahasa Indonesia sedikit.**
I can speak a little Indonesian.

4 **tidak bisa**
cannot

38 **Tanah airku India. Saya tidak bisa bicara bahasa Indonesia.**
My homeland is India. I cannot speak Indonesian.

5 **sedikit**
a little

Additional Vocabulary

13 **lahir**
born

14 **kota; desa**
city; village

15 **negara**
country

16 **dari**
from

17 **tidak**
no; not (used with verbs/adjectives)

18 **bukan**
no; not (used with nouns)

19 **dapat; mendapat**
to get

20 **berbahasa**
to speak a language

21 **bicara; berbicara**
to speak

22 **asalnya**
to come from

23 **keturunan**
descendants

24 **asli**
original; indigenous to a particular area

25 **alamat**
address

26 **tinggal**
to live

27 **nenek moyang**
ancestors

28 **orang**
person

29 **daerah**
area

30 **suku bangsa**
ethnic group

31 **budaya; kebudayaan**
culture

32 **penduduk**
resident; inhabitant

6 pakaian pengantin adat Yogyakarta
traditional wedding costume of Yogyakarta

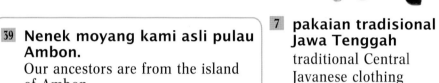

39 **Nenek moyang kami asli pulau Ambon.**
Our ancestors are from the island of Ambon.

7 **pakaian tradisional Jawa Tenggah**
traditional Central Javanese clothing

8 **pakaian pengantin adat Jawa Barat**
traditional wedding costume of West Java

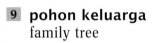
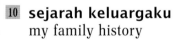

Pohon Keluarga
Sejarah Keluargaku

9 **pohon keluarga**
family tree

10 **sejarah keluargaku**
my family history

11 **adat**
custom

12 **pakaian**
clothing

40 **Apakah buku itu dalam bahasa Indonesia?**
Is that book in Indonesian?

41 **Bukan, buku ini berbahasa Inggris.**
No this is an English language book.

42 **Anda berasal dari negara mana?**
Which country do you come from?

43 **Saya berasal dari Singapura.**
I come from Singapore.

44 **Ayah mantan Presiden Obama berasal dari Afrika, ibunya dari Amerika Serikat dan bapak tirinya dari Indonesia.**
The father of former President Obama came from Africa, his mother from America and his stepfather from Indonesia.

45 **Pemain musik rok Alex dan Eddie van Halen punya darah Indonesia. Neneknya orang Jawa.**
The rock musicians Alex and Eddie van Halen have Indonesian ancestry. Their grandmother was Javanese.

33 Mau makan apa?
What do you want to eat?

1 **enak**
tasty; nice

2 **sedap**
delicious

3 **makan**
to eat

4 **mie**
noodles

5 **tusuk saté**
satay skewers

6 **saté**
satay

7 **gado-gado**
cooked vegetables
with peanut sauce

8 **masak; memasak**
to cook

9 **masakan**
cooking

10 **bakar**
chargrilled (lit. burned)

11 **ayam bakar**
grilled chicken

12 **panggang**
roasted

13 **goreng**
fried

14 **rebus**
steamed

15 **tahu**
tofu

16 **lumpia**
spring rolls

17 **sambal manis pedas**
sweet chili sauce

18 **mie goreng**
fried noodles

19 **ayam goreng**
fried chicken

20 **nasi campur**
steamed rice with mixed
meat and vegetables

21 **cabai**
chili

22 **rendang**
slow-cooked beef in
coconut and spices

23 **tempe**
fermented soya
bean cakes

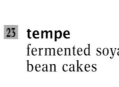

24 **soto ayam**
spicy chicken broth

25 nasi
steamed rice

26 porsi
portion

27 kangkung
water spinach

28 ikan goreng
fried fish

29 makanan
food

30 manisan
sweets; desserts

34 piring kosong
empty plate

35 sumpit
chopsticks

36 sendok
spoon

37 garpu
fork

31 taoge
bean sprouts

32 sayur
vegetables

33 ketimun
cucumber

38 pisau
knife

41 kue lapis
layer cake

40 bubur ketan hitam
sweet black sticky
rice (with coconut
milk)

39 dadar gulung
green pancakes
with coconut and
palm sugar

Additional Vocabulary

42 sop
soup

43 santan
coconut milk

44 pilihan
choice

45 istimewa
special

46 juga
also

47 garam
salt

48 merica
pepper

49 manis
sweet

50 asam
sour

51 pedas
spicy hot

52 panas
hot (heat)

53 pahit
bitter

54 lagi
more

55 tambah lagi
to have some more

56 pisang goreng
fried bananas

57 nasi goreng
fried rice

58 telur dadar
omelette

59 gulai; gule
spicy curry

60 Saya suka makan nasi goreng.
I like eating fried rice.

61 Kami makan nasi tiga kali sehari.
We eat rice three times a day.

34 Mau minum apa?
What do you want to drink?

4 jeruk peras freshly squeezed orange juice

3 es cola iced cola

50 Saya suka minum es alpukat.
I like to drink iced avocado shakes.

1 minum to drink

2 minuman a drink

5 es kopi iced coffee

6 jus juice

7 jus semangka watermelon juice

8 es jeruk iced citrus drink

9 es cendol iced coconut milk with palm sugar and jellies

10 es kelapa muda young coconut water

11 jahe hangat warm ginger drink

12 teh tea

13 kopi (tanpa susu) coffee (without milk)

14 kopi susu milk coffee

15 es teh iced tea

16 teh botol bottled sweet tea

17 teh hijau green tea

18 air (pronounced "a-yir") water

19 air mineral mineral water

 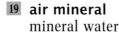

20 kopi tubruk mud coffee

45 **Saya mau pesan minuman. Satu kopi dan satu air mineral.**
I would like to order drinks. One coffee and one mineral water.

46 **Kopinya pakai es atau panas?**
Iced coffee or hot coffee?

47 **Pakai es.**
Iced coffee.

48 **Kopi tubruk adalah kopi khas Indonesia.**
Mud coffee is traditional Indonesian-style coffee.

49 **Jangan minum air keran di Indonesia.**
Don't drink tap water in Indonesia.

Susu kedelai
segar dan bergizi

- menguatkan tulang
- bebas kolesterol
- memberikan energi

21 **minuman keras**
alcohol drinks

22 **anggur**
wine; grapes

23 **pakai**
to use

24 **susu kedelai**
soya milk

25 **bergizi**
nutritious

27 **anggur merah dan anggur putih**
red wine and white wine

26 **bir**
beer

28 **brem**
sweet rice wine

Additional Vocabulary

29 **haus**
thirsty

30 **es**
ice

31 **jahe**
ginger

32 **panas**
hot

33 **dingin**
cold

34 **air putih (rebus)**
pure boiled water

35 **gelas**
glass

36 **cangkir**
cup

37 **gula**
sugar

38 **tanpa gula**
without sugar

39 **pakai gula**
with sugar

40 **susu**
milk

41 **tanpa susu**
without milk

42 **susu coklat**
chocolate milk

43 **warung kopi**
coffee shop

44 **biji kopi**
coffee beans

35 | Kita akan makan di mana?
Where shall we eat?

1 makan di luar
to eat out

3 rumah makan
restaurant
(usually basic)

2 restoran
restaurant

33 Kami makan di mal.
We are eating in the mall.

4 pedagang kaki lima
street seller
(on wheels)

5 bubur ayam
chicken porridge

6 warung
roadside food stall

7 pasar malam
night market

10 martabak
egg, onion, mince meat
fried in thin crispy dough

8 mie ayam dan bakso
chicken noodles with meatballs

9 bakso
meatball soup

36 Sudah makan belum?
Have you eaten?
Sudah. **Belum.**
Already. (Yes)   Not yet. (No)

37 Apakah Anda pernah mencoba masakan Padang?
Have you ever tried Padang food?

38 Mau makan pisang goreng di pasar malam?
Do you want to eat fried bananas at the night market?

34 **Bolehkah saya memesan sarapan ala barat.**
May I order a Western breakfast?

35 **Boleh saja!**
Of course you can!

11 **sarapan barat**
Western breakfast

12 **jus buah-buahan**
juice

13 **kopi**
coffee

14 **sereal**
cereal

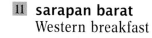

15 **telur mata sapi**
sunny side up eggs

16 **roti panggang**
toast

17 **roti**
bread

19 **telur**
eggs

20 **keju**
cheese

18 **selai**
jam

21 **makan cepat saji**
fastfood

22 **kafe modern**
modern cafe

23 **nasi bungkus**
a boxed meal to go

24 **nasi gudeg**
a Yogyakarta speciality made from young jackfruit

39 **Cafe Batavia adalah restoran terkenal di Jakarta.**
Cafe Batavia is a famous restaurant in Jakarta.

Additional Vocabulary

25 **pelayan**
waiter

26 **pesan; memesan**
to order; book

27 **lauk-pauk**
side dishes

28 **sarapan; makan pagi**
breakfast

29 **makan siang**
lunch

30 **makan malam**
dinner

31 **daftar makanan**
menu

32 **rumah makan Cina**
Chinese restaurant

36 Beli buah-buahan
Buying fruits

1 kelapa
coconut

2 pisang
banana(s)

3 rambutan
rambutan(s)

4 kelapa muda
young coconut(s)

5 durian
durian

6 nanas
pineapple

7 persik
peach(es)

8 pepaya
paw-paw;
papaya

9 jeruk limun
lemon

10 jeruk nipis
lime

11 jeruk Bali
pomelo

12 lengkeng
longan

13 stroberi
strawberry

14 anggur
grapes

> **39 Buah ini enak!**
> This fruit is delicious!

15 belewah
cantaloupe

16 kesemek
persimmon

17 semangka
watermelon

18 nangka
jackfruit

19 prem
plum(s)

20 pir
pear(s)

21 apel
apple(s)

22 mangga
mango

23 belimbing
star fruit

24 manggis
mangosteen

25 salak
snake fruit(s)

33 Saya suka makan pisang.
I like eating bananas.

34 Berapa harga jambu ini, Pak?
How much are these jambu, Pak?

36 Mahal sekali! Tiga puluh dua ribu rupiah saja, ya?
Very expensive. Just Rp32,000, alright?

38 Ya, baiklah.
Ok, good.

35 Manis ini, Bu. Harganya empat puluh ribu rupiah.
These are sweet, Bu. Only Rp.40,000.

37 Tidak bisa, Bu. Tiga puluh lima ribu rupiah harga pasnya, Bu.
It's not possible, Bu. Rp.35,000 is the exact price.

26 jambu
rose apples

Additional Vocabulary

27 jus buah
fruit juice

30 segar
fresh

28 jeruk
citrus

31 matang
ripe; well-cooked

29 potong; memotong
to cut

32 mentah
unripe

81

37 Sayuran, kacang, dan bumbu-bumbu
Vegetables, nuts, and spices

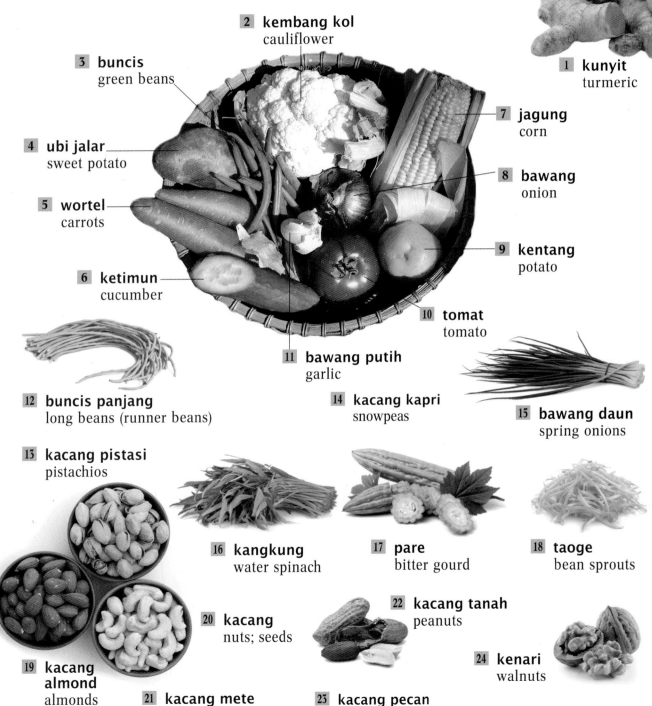

2 kembang kol
cauliflower

3 buncis
green beans

1 kunyit
turmeric

7 jagung
corn

4 ubi jalar
sweet potato

8 bawang
onion

5 wortel
carrots

9 kentang
potato

6 ketimun
cucumber

10 tomat
tomato

11 bawang putih
garlic

12 buncis panjang
long beans (runner beans)

14 kacang kapri
snowpeas

15 bawang daun
spring onions

13 kacang pistasi
pistachios

16 kangkung
water spinach

17 pare
bitter gourd

18 taoge
bean sprouts

22 kacang tanah
peanuts

20 kacang
nuts; seeds

24 kenari
walnuts

19 kacang almond
almonds

21 kacang mete
cashew nuts

23 kacang pecan
pecan nuts

25 jinten
cumin

26 jahe
ginger

27 lengkuas; laos
galangal

28 daun jeruk purut
kaffir lime leaves

29 serai
lemongrass

30 daun ketumbar
coriander leaves;
cilantro

31 pala
nutmeg

32 cengkeh
cloves

33 kayu manis
cinnamon

34 ketumbar
coriander

35 cabai rawit
small very hot chilies

36 cabai merah
red chilies

37 paprika
bell pepper

38 kemiri
candlenuts

39 alu dan lumpang
pestle and mortar

Additional Vocabulary

41 alergi
allergy

42 kacang polong
peas

43 kubis
cabbage

44 bawang merah
shallots

45 bayam
spinach

**46 tumbuk;
menumbuk**
ground; to grind

47 Saya suka makan sayur.
I like to eat vegetables.

48 Anda suka kacang apa?
What nuts do you like?

49 Saya suka kacang mete.
I like cashew nuts.

40 pasar apung
floating market (Banjarmasin)

50 Saya alergi kacang.
I am allergic to nuts.

51 Biji ketumbar ditumbuk sebelum dimasak.
Coriander seeds are ground before cooking.

38 | Di pasar dan di toko
At the market and at the store

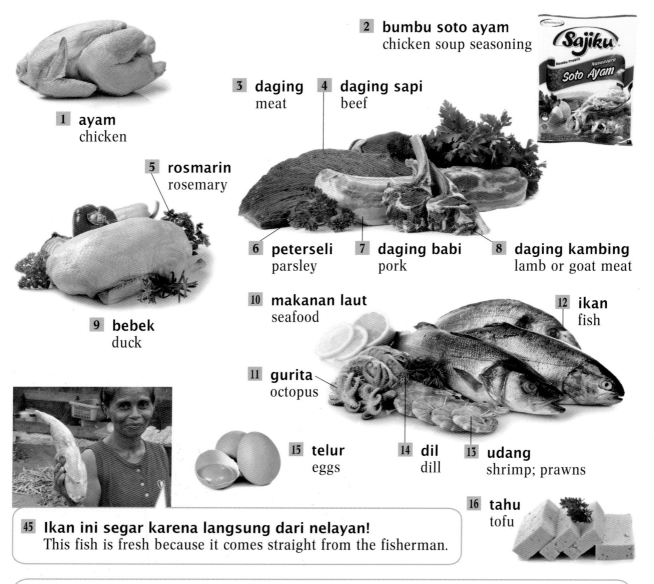

1 ayam
chicken

2 bumbu soto ayam
chicken soup seasoning

3 daging
meat

4 daging sapi
beef

5 rosmarin
rosemary

6 peterseli
parsley

7 daging babi
pork

8 daging kambing
lamb or goat meat

9 bebek
duck

10 makanan laut
seafood

11 gurita
octopus

12 ikan
fish

13 udang
shrimp; prawns

14 dil
dill

15 telur
eggs

16 tahu
tofu

45 Ikan ini segar karena langsung dari nelayan!
This fish is fresh because it comes straight from the fisherman.

46 Di Indonesia, kami suka belanja di pasar karena lebih segar dan lebih murah.
In Indonesia, we like to shop at the market because it is fresher and cheaper.

47 Tetapi, di pasar harus tawar-menawar.
However, at the market you have to bargain.

22 krupuk udang
shrimp crackers

20 **sambal**
chili sauce

21 **saus tomat**
tomato sauce (ketchup)

23 **mie instan**
instant noodles

17 **kecap manis**
sweet soy sauce

18 **kecap asin**
regular soy sauce

19 **kaleng (kalengan)**
can (canned)

24 **dodol**
a candy made from sticky
rice flour and fruit

25 **biskuit**
biscuits

Additional Vocabulary

26 **garam dan merica**
salt and pepper

27 **keripik singkong**
cassava chips

28 **tepung sagu**
sago flour

29 **tepung**
flour

30 **minyak goreng** cooking oil	**38** **sebelum** before
31 **minyak kacang** peanut oil	**39** **sebelumnya** beforehand
32 **minyak kelapa** coconut oil	**40** **sesudah** after
33 **minyak kelapa sawit** palm oil	**41** **sesudahnya** afterwards
34 **minyak zaitun** olive oil	**42** **masakan khas** a specialty 'dish'
35 **langsung** directly	**43** **pancing; memancing** to fish
36 **goreng; mengoreng** to fry	**44** **nelayan** fisherman
37 **saus kacang** peanut sauce	

48 **Papeda adalah masakan khas Ambon yang dibuat dari tepung sagu.**
Papeda is a special dish from Ambon
which is made from sago flour.

Kata-kata yang berguna
Useful words

Questions

1 Siapa?
Who?

2 Apa?
What?

3 Kapan?
When?

4 Di mana?
Where?

5 Ke mana?
Where to?

6 Kenapa?/Mengapa?
Why?

7 Bagaimana?
How?

8 Berapa?
How many?

9 Berapa lama?
How long? (time)

10 Berapa jauh?
How far?

11 Siapa nama Anda?
What is your name?

12 Berapa umur Anda?
How old are you?

13 Berapa harganya?
How much is it?

14 Jam berapa?
What time is it?

15 Berasal dari mana?
Where do you come from?

16 Naik apa?
What do I travel by?

Being polite

17 Terima kasih.
Thank you.

18 Sama-sama.
You're welcome.

19 Apa kabar?
How are you?

20 Kabar baik.
I'm well.

21 Permisi...
Excuse me...

22 Boleh saya...
May I....

23 Maaf.
Sorry.

24 Tolong ulangi lagi.
Please repeat.

25 Minta tolong.
Could you help me.

26 Saya tidak mengerti.
I don't understand.

Other Expressions

27 Bagus!
That's great!

28 Awas!
Watch out!

29 Ada apa?
What's up?

30 Bagaimana?
Pardon?; How?

31 Tidak apa-apa.
It's ok (I don't mind).

32 Di mana WC?
Where is the toilet?

33 Hati-hati!
Be careful!

34 Sekali lagi.
Say it again (lit.one more time).

35 Selamat jalan! Sampai bertemu lagi!
Safe travels! See you soon!

English-Indonesian Index

The following information is included for each entry–the English word, the Indonesian word, the section number and the order in which the word appeared in that section, followed by the page number where the word appears. For example:

English word	Indonesian word	Lesson and order	Page in book
car	**mobil**	[12-1]	32

browser **peramban** [22-22] 52
Brunei **Brunei** [31-21] 70
Buddha's birthday **Hari Raya Waisak** [18-18] 44
Buddhism **agama Budha** [18-16] 44
building **gedung** [11-2] 30
bus **bis; bus** [12-12] 33
bus route **rute bis** [12-30] 33
bus stop **halte bus; tempat perhentian bus** [12-33] 33
business **bisnis** [24-24] 57
busy **ramai** [11-6] 30
but **tetapi** [31-64] 71
butterfly **kupu-kupu** [28-29] 65
by one's self **sendiri** [22-17] 52

C
CD/DVD **CD/DVD** [22-11] 52
cabbage **kubis** [37-43] 83
cable **kabel** [22-63] 53
calculator **kalkulator** [5-16] 19; [20-13] 48
calendar **kalender** [16-1] 40
Cambodia **Kamboja** [31-9] 70
camera **kamera** [30-11] 68
can (tin) **kaleng** [38-19] 85
can (to be able) **bisa** [32-3] 72
Canada **Kanada** [31-34] 71
candlenuts **kemiri** [37-38] 83
canned **kalengan** [38-19] 85
cannot **tidak bisa** [32-4] 72
cantaloupe **belewah** [36-15] 80
capital city **ibu kota** [31-54] 71
car **mobil** [12-1] 32
carpenter **tukang kayu** [24-42] 57
carpet **karpet** [3-8] 14
carrot(s) **wortel** [37-5] 82
carving **ukiran** [25-19] 59
cash **tunai** [9-8] 26
cashew nuts **kacang mete** [37-21] 82
cashier **kasir** [10-27] 29
cassava chips **keripik singkong** [38-26] 85
cat **kucing** [28-25] 65
Catholic religion **agama Katolik** [18-28] 45
caught in the rain **terjebak dalam hujan** [14-36] 37
caught out in the dark **kemalaman** [14-37] 37
cauliflower **kembang kol** [37-2] 82
ceiling **langit-langit** [3-4] 14
Celebrating the five governing principles of Indonesia (June 1) **Hari Kesaktian Pancasila (Tanggal 1 Juni)** [19-21] 47
celebration **perayaan** [19-24] 47
central business district (CBD) **pusat kawasan bisnis** [11-26] 31
Central Javanese gamelan **Gamelan Jawa** [25-9] 58
century **abad** [16-47] 41
cereal **sereal** [35-14] 79
ceremony **upacara** [18-33] 45
chair **kursi** [3-14] 14
change (from a purchase) **uang kembali** [9-15] 27; [10-41] 29
chargrilled (lit. burned) **bakar** [33-10] 74
chat room **ruang obrolan** [22-60] 53
cheap **murah** [9-24] 27; [10-37] 29
cheaper **lebih murah** [10-38] 29
check; cheque **cek** [9-18] 27
cheek **pipi** [4-9] 16
cheese **keju** [35-20] 79
chef **koki; juru masak** [24-16] 57

chemistry **ilmu kimia** [20-8] 48; [21-38] 51
chest **dada** [4-30] 17
chicken **ayam** [28-22] 65; [38-1] 84
chicken noodles with meatballs **mie ayam dan bakso** [35-8] 78
chicken porridge **bubur ayam** [35-5] 78
chicken soup seasoning **bumbu soto ayam** [38-2] 84
child **anak** [2-2] 12
children **anak-anak** [2-7] 12
chili **cabai** [33-21] 74
chili sauce **sambal** [38-20] 85
chin **dagu** [4-13] 16
China **Cina** [31-10] 70
Chinese New Year **Tahun Baru Imlek** [19-19] 47
Chinese restaurant **rumah makan Cina** [35-32] 79
chocolate **coklat** [19-16] 47
chocolate milk **susu coklat** [34-42] 77
choice **pilihan** [33-44] 75
chopsticks **sumpit** [33-35] 75
Christmas **Hari Natal** [18-32] 45
Christmas tree **pohon Natal** [19-14] 47
church **gereja** [18-30] 45
cinema **bioskop** [11-30] 31
cinnamon **kayu manis** [37-33] 83
citrus **jeruk** [36-28] 81
city; village **kota; desa** [32-14] 72
city center **pusat kota** [11-25] 31
class at university **kuliah** [20-25] 49
classmates **teman sekelas** [20-14] 48
classroom **ruang kelas** [20-4] 48
clean **bersih** [8-11] 24; [27-26] 63
clean energy **tenaga bersih** [27-24] 63
clear (sky) **cerah** [14-6] 36
climate change **perubahan iklim** [27-47] 63
climb mountains **naik gunung** [29-21] 67
closed **tutup** [8-15] 25
clothes **pakaian** [10-7] 28; [30-2] 68
clothing **pakaian** [32-12] 73
clothing size **ukuran pakaian** [7-29] 23
cloud(s) **awan** [14-20] 37; [26-27] 61
cloudy day **berawan** [14-7] 36
cloves **cengkeh** [37-32] 83
cockatoo **kakatua** [28-4] 64
coconut **kelapa** [26-23] 61; [36-1] 80
coconut milk **santan** [33-43] 75
coconut oil **minyak kelapa** [38-32] 85
coffee **kopi** [35-13] 79; (without milk) **kopi (tanpa susu)** [34-13] 76
coffee beans **biji kopi** [34-44] 77
coffee shop **warung kopi** [34-43] 77
coins **koin** [9-3] 26
cold **dingin** [14-18] 37; [34-33] 77
color(s) **warna** [7-1] 22
communications **komunikasi** [21-45] 51
community **masyarakat** [27-13] 62
company **perusahaan** [24-22] 57
comparing prices **perbandingan harga** [10-30] 29
computer **komputer** [22-2] 52
computer mouse **tetikus** [22-7] 52
conference center **gedung konferensi** [11-11] 30

connection **sambungan** [22-56] 53
cooked vegetables with peanut sauce **gado-gado** [33-7] 74
cooking **masakan** [33-9] 74
cooking oil **minyak goreng** [38-30] 85
cooking utensils **alat memasak** [3-26] 15
cool **sejuk** [14-32] 37
copy/paste **salin/tempel** [22-36] 53
copyright **hak cipta** [22-67] 53
coriander **ketumbar** [37-34] 83
coriander leaves; cilantro **daun ketumbar** [37-30] 83
corn **jagung** [37-7] 82
cosmetics **kosmetik** [10-23] 29
cousin(s) **sepupu** [2-23] 13
country **negara** [32-15] 72
country code **kode negara** [23-22] 54
cow **sapi** [28-18] 65
crater **kawah** [26-43] 61
credit card **kartu kredit** [9-17] 27
cremation (in Balinese: ngaben) **kremasi** [18-26] 45
crocodile **buaya** [28-14] 65
cucumber **ketimun** [33-33] 75; [37-6] 82
culture **budaya; kebudayaan** [32-31] 72
cumin **jinten** [37-25] 83
cup **cangkir** [34-36] 77
cupboard **lemari** [3-27] 15
currency **mata uang** [9-7] 26
curtain **tirai** [3-17] 14
cushion **bantal** [3-10] 14
custom **adat** [32-11] 73
customs **bea cukai** [31-56] 71

D
dancer **penari** [25-1] 58
dangerous **berbahaya** [8-21] 25
dark blue **biru tua** [7-15] 22
date **tanggal** [16-6] 40
day **hari** [16-4] 40
daughter **anak perempuan** [2-6] 12
daughter-in-law **menantu perempuan** [2-38] 12
debt **utang** [9-28] 27
decade **darsawarsa** [16-46] 41
December **Desember** [16-29] 41
degree **gelar** [20-40] 49
degrees (temp) **derajat** [14-31] 37
delicious **sedap** [33-2] 74
delivery cost **biaya pengiriman** [10-29] 29
delivery van **mobil pengiriman** [12-7] 32
Denmark **Denmark** [31-35] 71
dentist **dokter gigi** [17-26] 43; [24-40] 57
design **desain** [22-58] 53
department store **toko serba ada** [10-26] 29
desk **meja tulis** [3-37] 15
diary **buku harian** [16-5] 40
dictionary **kamus** [21-9] 50
difficult **sulit** [8-18] 25
digestion **pencernaan** [4-36] 17
digit; digit **angka** [5-29] 19
diligent **rajin** [21-46] 51
dill **dil** [38-14] 84
dinner **makan malam** [35-30] 79
direction **arah** [13-10] 35
directly **langsung** [38-35] 85

dirty **kotor** [8-11] 24; [27-27] 63
discount **diskon** [9-22] 27
distance **jarak** [13-11] 35
dizzy **pusing** [17-39] 43
doctor **dokter** [17-2] 42; [24-19] 57
doctor's certificate **surat dokter** [17-51] 43
doctor's practice **praktek dokter** [17-27] 43
dog **anjing** [28-24] 65
dolphin **lumba-lumba** [28-43] 65
don't **jangan** [27-33] 63
don't worry **jangan khawatir** [17-48] 43
door **pintu** [3-9] 14
dosage **takaran** [17-44] 43
down **turun** [8-6] 24
dragonfly **capung** [28-27] 65
drawer **laci** [3-33] 15
driver **sopir** [12-4] 32
drums **kendang** [25-12] 58
dry season **musim kemarau** [26-7] 60
duck **bebek** [28-39] 65; [38-9] 84
durian **durian** [36-5] 80
during **selama** [16-49] 41; [27-19] 62
dye **pewarna** [25-21] 59

E
e-magazine **e-majalah** [22-20] 52
ear **telinga** [4-5] 16
ear, nose and throat **telingga, hidung dan tenggorokan** [17-28] 43
early **awal** [15-24] 39
early morning **pagi-pagi** [26-28] 61
earth **tanah** [27-3] 62
earthquake **gempa bumi** [26-48] 61
east **timur** [13-18] 35
East Timor (Timor Leste) **Timor Timur** [31-20] 70
Easter **Paskah** [18-31] 45
easy **mudah** [8-18] 25
economics **ekonomi** [21-36] 51
education **pendidikan** [21-48] 51
egg, onion, mince meat fried in thin crispy dough **martabak** [35-10] 78
eggs **telur** [35-19] 79; [38-15] 84
eight **delapan** [5-8] 18
elbow **siku** [4-26] 17
electric car **mobil listrik** [27-22] 63
electrician **tukang listrik** [24-4] 56
elephant **gajah** [28-13] 65
email **surel; email** [22-12] 52
emergency **keadaan darurat** [17-37] 43
emergency room **ruang darurat** [17-6] 42
employee **karyawan** [24-28] 57
employer **majikan** [24-27] 57
empty plate **piring kosong** [33-34] 75
end of the fasting month **Lebaran** [18-9] 44
engineer **insinyur** [24-5] 56
English language **bahasa Inggris** [31-16] 70
enjoyable **menyenangkan** [29-35] 67
enter **masuk** [8-10] 24
entrepreneur **pengusaha** [24-23] 57
environment; surroundings **lingkungan** [26-2] 60
environmental conservation **pelestarian lingkungan** [27-45] 63

equals **sama dengan** [5-21] 19
eraser **penghapus** [21-17] 51
eruption **letusan** [26-39] 61
ethnic group **suku bangsa** [32-30] 72
Europe **Eropa** [31-29] 71
even numbers **angka genap** [5-25] 19
exam **ujian** [21-3] 50
exchange rate **kurs** [9-19] 27
exhibition **pameran** [25-39] 59
exit **keluar** [8-10] 24
expensive **mahal** [9-25] 27; [10-35] 29
expressway **jalan tol** [11-22] 31
extinct; extinction **punah; kepunahan** [27-18] 62
eye **mata** [4-4] 16
eyebrow **alis** [4-3] 16

F
face **wajah** [4-10] 16
family **keluarga** [2-25] 12
family name **nama keluarga** [1-25] 11
family tree **pohon keluarga** [32-9] 73
famous **terkenal** [25-33] 59
fan **kipas angin** [3-18] 14
far **jauh** [8-23] 25; [13-14] 35
farmer **petani** [24-11] 56
fast/strong wind **angin kencang** [14-30] 37
fast **cepat** [8-24] 25
faster **lebih cepat** [12-23] 33
fastfood **makan cepat saji** [35-21] 79
fasting month **Ramadan; bulan puasa** [18-2] 44; [18-8] 44
fat **gemuk** [8-4] 24
father **bapak** [2-12] 13; father (Mr.) **bapak (pak)** [2-29] 12
Fathers Day **Hari Ayah** [19-11] 46
February **Februari** [16-19] 41
female **wanita** [2-4] 12
fermented soya bean cakes **tempe** [33-23] 74
fever **demam** [17-15] 42
field of study **bidang** [20-36] 49
fierce **buas** [28-33] 65
fifteen minutes past six **jam enam lewat lima belas menit** [15-9] 38
fifty thousand rupiah note **uang lima puluh ribu rupiah** [9-13] 26
file **dokumen** [22-54] 53
finally **pada akhirnya** [15-35] 39
fingers **jari tangan** [4-15] 16
Finland **Finlandia** [31-36] 71
fire engine mobil **pemadam kebakaran** [12-16] 33
fireworks **kembang api** [19-18] 47
first aid **pertolongan pertama** [17-52] 43
fish **ikan** [28-30] 65; [38-12] 84
fisherman **nelayan** [38-44] 85
five **lima** [5-5] 18
five minutes past six **jam enam lewat lima menit** [15-5] 38
five minutes to seven **jam tujuh kurang lima menit** [15-12] 38
five thousand rupiah note **uang lima ribu rupiah** [9-10] 26
fixed price **harga pas** [9-23] 27
floating market **pasar apung** [37-40] 83
flora; plants **tumbuhan** [26-45] 61

flora and fauna **tumbuhan dan hewan** [27-4] 62
flood **banjir** [14-17] 37
floor **lantai** [3-20] 14
floors/levels **lantai/tingkat** [3-56] 14
flour **tepung** [38-29] 85
flower **bunga** [26-13] 60
fog **kabut** [14-21] 37
food **makanan** [33-29] 75
for; in order to **untuk** [30-49] 69
for rent **disewakan** [3-63] 14
for sale **dijual** [3-58] 14
forehead **dahi** [4-23] 17
foreign currency **valuta asing** [9-39] 27
foreign language **bahasa asing** [21-5] 50
forest; jungle **hutan** [26-19] 60
fork **garpu** [33-37] 75
formula **rumus** [5-31] 19
four **empat** [5-4] 18
fraction **pecahan** [5-24] 19
France **Prancis** [31-37] 71
frangipani **kemboja** [26-10] 60
free **bebas** [23-27] 55
free internet connection **koneksi internet gratis** [31-59] 71
free time **waktu luang** [6-30] 20
fresh **segar** [36-30] 81
freshly squeezed orange juice **jeruk peras** [34-4] 76
frequently **sering** [15-33] 39
Friday **hari Jumat** [16-16] 40
fried **goreng** [33-13] 74
fried bananas **pisang goreng** [33-56] 75
fried chicken **ayam goreng** [33-19] 74
fried fish **ikan goreng** [33-28] 75
fried noodles **mie goreng** [33-18] 74
fried rice **nasi goreng** [33-57] 75
friend(s) **teman** [1-37] 11
frog **kodok** [28-38] 65
from **dari** [13-44] 35; [32-16] 72
front **depan** [8-22] 25
frontyard **halaman depan** [3-61] 14
fruit juice **jus buah** [36-27] 81
full (with food) **kenyang** [8-31] 25
funny; cute **lucu** [28-32] 65

G
galangal **lengkuas; laos** [37-27] 83
garage **garasi** [3-59] 14
garden **taman** [3-6] 14
gardener **tukang kebun** [24-20] 57
garlic **bawang putih** [37-11] 82
gathering; meeting **pertemuan** [1-20] 11
gecko (house lizard) **cicak** [28-37] 65
gendèr (musical instrument) **gendèr** [25-7] 58
geography **geografi** [21-40] 51
Germany **Jerman** [31-38] 71
get well quickly **cepat sembuh** [17-46] 43
getting to know someone **berkenalan** [1-7] 10
gift; present **hadiah** [19-15] 47
ginger **jahe** [34-31] 77; [37-26] 83
giraffe **jerapah** [28-11] 64
glass **gelas** [34-35] 77
glasses; spectacles **kaca mata** [10-22] 29
global warming **pemanasan global** [27-48] 63
go straight **terus; lurus** [12-27] 33
go straight ahead **lurus** [13-8] 34

goat **kambing** [28-16] 65
God **Tuhan** [18-37] 45
gold **emas** [7-13] 22
golf **golf** [29-17] 66
gong **gong** [25-13] 58
good **baik** [8-7] 24
Good afternoon (from 3pm to 6pm) **Selamat sore** [1-10] 10
Good-bye (said by the person leaving to the people staying) **Selamat tinggal** [1-18] 11
Good-bye... (said by the people staying behind) **Selamat jalan...** [1-19] 11
good-bye ("safe journey" to someone leaving) **selamat jalan** [1-30] 11
good-bye ("safe stay" to those staying) **selamat tinggal** [1-29] 11
Good day (noon up to 3pm) **Selamat siang** [1-9] 10
Good morning (up to midday) **Selamat pagi** [1-8] 10
Good-night/evening **Selamat malam** [1-11] 10
good weather **cuaca baik** [14-28] 37
goods; things **barang** [10-42] 29
grade; class **kelas** [21-22] 51
grades **nilai** [20-28] 49
graduated **diwisuda** [20-55] 49
graduation **wisuda** [20-55] 49
graduation day **hari wisuda** [20-44] 49
grandfather **kakek** [2-8] 13
grandmother **nenek** [2-9] 13
grandson; granddaughter **cucu** [2-30] 12
grapes **anggur** [36-14] 80
grass **rumput** [26-30] 61
gray **abu-abu** [7-10] 22
Great Britain **Inggris** [31-39] 71
green **hijau** [7-7] 22
green beans **buncis** [37-3] 82
green pancakes with coconut and palm sugar **dadar gulung** [33-39] 75
green tea **teh hijau** [34-17] 76
greeting **salam** [1-39] 11
grilled chicken **ayam bakar** [33-11] 74
groom **pengantin laki-laki** [19-27] 47
ground; to grind **tumbuk; menumbuk** [37-46] 83
guide **pemandu** [30-38] 69
guest; visitor **tamu** [1-23] 11; [31-62] 71
guitar **gitar** [25-3] 58

H
hail **hujan es** [14-23] 37
hail a taxi **panggil taksi** [12-31] 33
hair **rambut** [4-1] 16
hairbrush **sikat rambut** [30-3] 68
hairdresser **penata rambut** [24-10] 56
half **setengah** [15-8] 38
half past six **jam setengah tujuh** [15-10] 38
hand **tangan** [4-24] 17
happy **senang** [8-5] 24
Happy New Year! **Selamat Tahun Baru!** [19-4] 46
hat **topi** [10-17] 28; [30-6] 68
head **kepala** [4-2] 16
headache **sakit kepala** [17-22] 43
headphones **pelantang** [30-8] 68
health **kesehatan** [4-49] 17; [29-29] 67
healthy **sehat** [4-47] 17; [29-30] 67

heart **antung** [4-19] 17
herbal drinks seller **penjual jamu** [17-57] 43
herbal remedy **jamu** [17-56] 43
here **di sini** [13-21] 35
high **tinggi** [8-28] 25
high blood pressure **tekanan darah tinggi** [17-17] 42
highlighter **stabilo** [21-15] 51
hijab (head covering) **jilbab** [10-19] 29
Hindu religion **agama Hindu** [18-19] 45
Hindu-Bali temple **pura** [18-22] 45
history **sejarah** [21-34] 51
hobby **hobi** [6-37] 20; [29-37] 67
holiday **libur; liburan** [16-50] 41; [30-37] 69
home delivery **pengiriman ke rumah** [10-28] 29
homeland **tanah air** [32-2] 72
homepage **beranda** [22-18] 52
homework **pekerjaan rumah** [21-27] 51
horse **kuda** [28-19] 65
horse cart **dokar** [12-8] 32
hospital **rumah sakit** [17-4] 42
hot **panas** [14-9] 36; [33-52] 75; [34-32] 77
hotel **hotel** [11-15] 30; [30-17] 68
hour **jam** [15-1] 38
house **rumah** [11-31] 31
How are things going? **Bagaimana kabarnya?** [1-36] 11
How long? **Berapa lama?** [13-26] 35
humid **lembab** [14-10] 36
however **akan tetapi** [27-40] 63
hungry **lapar** [8-31] 25
husband and wife **suami dan istri** [2-13] 13
husband **suami** [2-32] 12

I
I; me **saya** [2-19] 13
I/my (formal) **saya** [2-41] 12; (informal) **aku** [2-42] 12
I'll be going now (to take one's leave) **saya pergi dulu** [1-35] 11
ice **es** [34-30] 77
iced citrus drink **es jeruk** [34-8] 76
iced coconut milk with palm sugar and jellies **es cendol** [34-9] 76
iced coffee **es kopi** [34-5] 76
iced cola **es cola** [34-3] 76
iced tea **es teh** [34-15] 76
if **kalau; jikalau** [27-42] 63
ill **sakit** [4-45] 17
illness **kesakitan** [4-46] 17
image (picture) **gambar** [22-37] 53
impact **dampak** [27-39] 63
important **penting** [17-50] 43
in a moment **sebentar** [15-34] 39
in the past **dahulu** [15-32] 39
including **termasuk** [22-66] 53
Independence Day **Hari Kemerdekaan** [19-20] 47
India **India** [31-6] 70
Indian Ocean **Samudra Hindia** [31-53] 71
Indonesian flag **bendera Indonesia** [19-1] 46
Indonesian language **bahasa Indonesia** [31-17] 70
Indonesian self defence **pencak silat** [29-18] 67
information technology **teknologi informasi** [21-32] 51

90

opportunity **kesempatan** [24-36] 57

opposite; across from **seberang** [13-15] 35

orange **jingga** [7-11] 22

orangutan **orang utan** [28-1] 64

orangutan rehabilitation center **pusat rehabilitasi orang utan** [27-52] 63

orchestra **orkes** [25-34] 59

orchid **anggrek** [26-12] 60

organs **organ** [4-35] 17

original; indigenous to a particular area **asli** [32-24] 72

outside **di luar** [13-5] 34

oven **oven** [3-29] 15

over many years **bertahun-tahun** [16-42] 41

overcast **mendung** [14-33] 37

overcome by flood; flooded **kebanjiran** [14-34] 37

overcome by cold **kedinginan** [14-19] 37

overcome by heat **kepanasan** [14-11] 36

P

Ph.D **Doktor Filsafat** [20-47] 49

Pacific Ocean **Samudra Pasifik** [31-52] 71

painter **pelukis** [24-12] 56

painting **gambar** [3-15] 14

palm **palem** [26-22] 61

palm oil **minyak kelapa sawit** [38-33] 85

papaya **pepaya** [36-8] 80

parents **orangtua** [2-1] 12

park **taman** [26-24] 61

parsley **peterseli** [38-6] 80

passenger **penumpang** [12-32] 33

passport **paspor** [31-1] 70

password **kata sandi** [22-33] 53

patient **pasien** [17-3] 42

paw-paw **pepaya** [36-8] 80

peach **persik** [36-7] 80

peacock **merak** [28-21] 65

peanut oil **minyak kacang** [38-31] 85

peanut sauce **saus kacang** [38-37] 85

peanuts **kacang tanah** [37-22] 82

pear **pir** [36-20] 81

peas **kacang polong** [37-42] 83

pecan nuts **kacang pecan** [37-23] 82

pedestrian **pejalan kaki** [11-39] 31

pedestrian bridge **jembatan penyeberangan** [11-3] 30

pedestrian crossing **tempat penyeberangan** [11-40] 31

pedicab **becak** [12-11] 32

pen **pena** [21-14] 51

pencil **pensil** [21-16] 51

pencil sharpener **rautan pensil** [21-19] 51

pepper **merica** [33-48] 75

percent (%) **persen** [5-23] 19

performance **pertunjukan** [25-40] 59; [30-26] 69

persimmon **kesemek** [36-16] 80

person **orang** [5-32] 19; orang [32-28] 72

pestle and mortar **alu dan lumpang** [37-39] 83

petrol station **pom bensin** [11-9] 30

pharmacist **apoteker** [24-9] 56

pharmacy **apotek** [17-33] 43

Philippines **Filipina** [31-22] 70

phone card **kartu telepon** [23-17] 54

phone charger **pengisi daya telepon** [23-16] 54

photo album **album foto** [22-26] 52

photocopier **mesin fotokopi** [20-9] 48

photographer **juru potret** [24-17] 57

physical education **ilmu jasmani** [21-42] 51

physics **ilmu fisika** [21-37] 51

physiotherapy **fisioterapi** [17-30] 43

pig **babi** [28-40] 65

pill **pil** [17-9] 42

pillow **bantal** [3-22] 14

pilot **pilot; penerbang** [24-18] 57

pineapple **nanas** [36-6] 80

pink **merah muda** [7-12] 22

pistachios **kacang pistasi** [37-13] 82

place **tempat** [13-39] 35; [27-11] 62

plastic bag **kantong plastik** [27-15] 62

Please forgive my sins **Mohon maaf lahir batin** [18-13] 44

please help **tolong bantu** [31-63] 71

plumber **tukang ledeng** [24-41] 57

plum **prem** [36-19] 81

police post **pos polisi** [11-21] 31

police station **kantor polisi** [11-42] 31

policeman **polisi** [24-7] 56

polluted **tercemar** [27-29] 63

pollution **polusi** [27-8] 62

pomelo **jeruk Bali** [36-11] 80

pop music **musik pop** [25-37] 59

population **populasi** [11-38] 31

portion **porsi** [33-26] 75

port **port** [12-15] 52

position **posisi** [24-37] 57

post office **kantor pos** [11-20] 31

potato **kentang** [37-9] 82

power socket **soket listrik** [3-54] 14

practice (noun) **latihan** [29-20] 67

praying at the temple **bersembahyang di pura** [18-23] 45

press clippings **kliping** [22-27] 52

prepaid phone **card kartu prabayar** [23-18] 54

primary school **sekolah dasar (SD)** [20-20] 49

private school **sekolah swasta** [20-32] 49

prescription **resep** [17-32] 43

price **harga** [9-21] 27

problem; issue **masalah** [21-26] 51

processional gamelan musicians **gamelan beleganjur** [18-27] 45

profile **profil** [22-25] 52

project **proyek** [23-15] 54

Protestant religion **agama Kristen** [18-29] 45

proud **bangga** [20-46] 49

public school **sekolah negeri** [20-33] 49

pull **tarik** [8-12] 24

punctual **tepat waktu** [15-23] 39

pure boiled water **air putih (rebus)** [34-54] 77

purple **ungu** [7-8] 22

purpose **maksud** [21-44] 51

push **dorong** [8-12] 24

Q

quarter **seperempat** [15-7] 38

question **pertanyaan** [21-53] 51

quick(ly) **cepat** [13-28] 35

quiet **sepi** [26-29] 61

R

racket **raket** [29-2] 66

rain; to rain **hujan** [14-5] 36

raincoat **jas hujan** [14-2] 36

rainbow **pelangi** [14-8] 36

rainstorm **hujan badai** [14-22] 37

rainy season **musim hujan** [26-6] 60

rambutan **rambutan** [36-3] 80

receipt **tanda terima** [9-37] 27

recycling **daur ulang** [27-23] 63

red **merah** [7-2] 22

red chilies **cabai merah** [37-36] 83

red rose **mawar merah** [19-17] 47

red wine and white wine **anggur merah dan anggur putih** [34-27] 77

refrigerator **kulkas** [3-28] 15

regular soy sauce **kecap asin** [38-18] 85

relatives **saudara** [2-33] 12

religion **agama** [18-15] 44

renewable energy **energi terbarukan** [27-23] 63

reservation **reservasi** [31-61] 71

resident; inhabitant **penduduk** [32-32] 72

resort **resor** [30-13] 68

restaurant **restoran** [35-2] 78; (usually basic) **rumah makan** [35-3] 78

result **akibat** [27-44] 63

return home **pulang** [1-38] 11

rhinoceros **badak** [28-3] 64

rice cakes boiled in woven coconut leaves **ketupat** [18-10] 44

rice fields **sawah** [26-36] 61

rice plant **padi** [26-38] 61

right **benar** [8-26] 25

ripe; well-cooked **matang** [36-31] 81

river **sungai** [26-18] 60

road; street **jalan** [11-4] 30

road (also to go) **jalan** [13-34] 35

roadside food stall **warung** [35-6] 78

roasted **panggang** [33-12] 74

Rock band **Band rock** [25-25] 59

roof **atap** [3-60] 15

room **kamar** [3-51] 14

rose apples **jambu** [36-26] 81

rosemary **rosmarin** [38-5] 84

rubbish **sampah** [27-9] 62

rugby **rugbi** [29-5] 66

ruler **penggaris** [21-20] 51

rupiah (the official currency of Indonesia) **rupiah** [9-1] 26

Russia **Rusia** [31-48] 71

S

S size **kecil** [7-31] 23

SIM card **kartu SIM** [23-19] 54

sad **sedih** [8-5] 24

safe **aman** [8-21] 25

sago flour **tepung sagu** [38-27] 85

sailing boat **perahu** [12-14] 33

salary **gaji** [24-45] 57

sale **obral** [10-39] 29

salt **garam** [33-47] 75

salt and pepper **garam dan merica** [38-25] 85

Same to you. (You're welcome.) **Sama-sama.** [1-22] 11

saron **saron** [25-10] 58

satay **saté** [33-6] 74

satay skewers **tusuk saté** [33-5] 74

Saturday **hari Sabtu** [16-17] 40

saved **tersimpan** [22-47] 53

savings **uang tabungan** [9-16] 27

scarf **syal** [10-21] 29

scholarship **beasiswa** [21-52] 51

school **sekolah** [20-17] 49

school principal **kepala sekolah** [20-27] 49

school subject **mata pelajaran** [20-24] 49

science **ilmu pengetahuan** [21-35] 51

science degree **gelar ilmu pengetahuan** [20-41] 49

scissors **gunting** [21-21] 51

screen **layar** [22-1] 52

sea **laut** [26-16] 60

seafood **makanan laut** [38-10] 84

season **musim** [26-5] 60

second(s) **detik** [15-3] 38

secretary **sekretaris** [24-15] 56

selfie **selfie** [23-2] 54

Senior high school **sekolah menengah atas (SMA)** [20-22] 49

September **September** [16-26] 41

server **peladen** [22-57] 53

settings **pengaturan; setelan** [22-70] 53

seven **tujuh** [5-7] 18

several times **beberapa kali** [17-43] 43

shadow puppet **wayang kulit** [25-31] 59

shallots **bawang merah** [37-44] 83

shape **bentuk** [7-38] 23

sheep **domba** [28-17] 65

shift work **kerja shift** [24-31] 57

ship **kapal** [12-13] 33

shoes **sepatu** [10-16] 28

shop(s) **toko** [10-25] 29; [11-24] 31

shopping bag **tas belanja** [10-4] 28

shopping center **pusat perbelanjaan** [11-28] 31

short **pendek** [8-2] 24; [8-3] 24

shoulder **bahu** [4-28] 17

shower **pancuran** [3-41] 15

shrimp; prawns **udang** [38-13] 84

shrimp crackers **krupuk udang** [38-22] 85

side dishes **lauk-pauk** [35-27] 79

sidewalk; pavement **trotoar** [11-35] 31

silver **perak** [7-14] 22

Singapore **Singapura** [31-15] 70

singer **penyanyi** [25-32] 59

sink **tempat cuci tangan** [3-39] 15

sister **saudara perempuan** [2-15] 13

sister-in-law **ipar perempuan** [2-36] 12

six **enam** [5-6] 18

size **ukuran** [7-39] 23

skeleton; frame **kerangka** [4-39] 17

skiing **berski** [29-9] 66

skin **kulit** [4-40] 17

skirt **rok** [10-13] 28

skyscraper **pencakar langit** [11-16] 30

slow **lambat** [8-24] 25

slow (down) **pelan-pelan** [12-22] 33

slow-cooked beef in coconut and spices **rendang** [33-22] 74

small **kecil** [7-37] 23; [8-14] 25

small change **uang kecil** [9-40] 27

small hotel **losmen** [30-40] 69

small very hot chilies **cabai rawit** [37-35] 83

smaller **lebih kecil** [7-41] 23

92

Photo Credits

The author would like to acknowledge the following friends and family for inclusion of their photos (first number refers to Theme, second to the number):

Aden (Hibbs) Bridge 33 (40); **Alan Hibbs** Endpapers (bajaj); 12 (10); **Arsiwi (Anna) Sutiyono** 29 (21); **Asita Majdi** Back cover; endpapers (nangka, keluarga kami, penjual jamu, Perkawinan Islam, Selamat belajar); Contents (boys singing, traditional clothing, nasi kuning, girl with mobile, becak); 1 (4–6, 12, 13); 2 (3–4, 5, 6, 45–47, 7–8 left, 9–23); 3 (48); 6 (3–6, 9–11, 15–16, 48); 7 (42, 44–45); 8 (1–2, 5-sad); 10 (1, 4, 19); 11 (10, 20, 21, 23, 48); 12 (8, 9, 11–12, 17, 37); 13 (1, 46, 50–51); 14 (1, 17, 18, 41); 39–43); 16 (53, 58, 59); 17 (7, 12, 57); 18 (1, 7, 10, 11, 17); 19 (6, 11, 12, 19, 22, 23); 20 (54); 23 (2, 13, 34, 36, 37); 24 (7, 11); 25 (3–4, 44, 45, 46); 26 (18, 19, 20, 33, 35, 39); 27 (Buang Sampah); 29 (12, 18); 30 (18, 24); 32 (33, 6, 7, 8); 33 (60); 33 (7, 16, 19, 22, 24, 25, 39, 41); 34 (3–9, 11, 16, 20); 35 (1, 2, 3, 4, 6, 23, 24); 36 (3–5, 11, 39, 25, 26, 33); 37 (12); 38 (46), page 85; **Barb Slee** 26 (7); **Denise Hibbs** 25 (19); **Eliza Henry Jones** 14 (21); 28 (16); 35 (17, 18); 36 (19, 20, 21); **Irene Ritchie** 28 (1); **Kris Williamson** 30 (22); **Linda Hibbs** Back cover; endpapers (kain dan kebaya), (Indonesian currency); Contents (wayang); p8; 1 (8–11); 3 (5); 8 (4, 6, 12); 9 (3–5, 15, 16); 10 (7–9, 12–13, 18); 14 (9); 16 (10); 18 (12); 19 (7, 8); 22 (13); 24 (6); 25 (7–15, 16, 23, 28, 29, 30); 26 (3, 8, 11, 12, 13, 14); 27 (Selamatkan Penyu); 32 (37); 33 (23, 60); 34 (26, 28); 37 (1–11, 26, 27, 28, 32, 34–39); 38 (17, 20, 22, 23); p86; **Michael Ewing** Endpapers (es kelapa muda, Ambon scene); Contents (girl drinking, Ambon scene); 2 (1); 11 (9, 22); 12 (16); 14 (7); 17 (58); 18 (21, 30); 25 (10); 26 (16, 17, 31); 27 (1, 8); 29 (19); 32 (39); 34 (10, 14, 50); 35 (39); 37 (31); 38 (45, 28, 48); **Michael Purwagani** 18 (14); 20 (55); 30 (13); **Michelle Purwagani** 14 (6); 19 (34); 26 (4); 30 (13, 43); 31 (68); 32 (34); 33 (1); **Robin Yulio** 19 (13); **Ruth Jackson** 28 (27); **Tracey Ferguson** Front flap; 13 (3, 47); 17 (18); 18 (24, 27); 30 (20); 32 (36); **Wendy Miller** Endpapers (penari Bali); 18 (27 single musician).

(Note: While all efforts have been made to trace and acknowledge copyright, the author and publishers tender their apologies for any accidental infringement where the original copyright has proved untraceable.)

Stock Photo Credits

Credits listed as follows: first number refers to Theme, second to the vocabulary number in that Theme.

Acknowledgments

The author would like to thank Asita Majdi in Yogyakarta for being such a wonderful friend over the years, and for her partnership in this project by not only taking a large number of photos specifically for the dictionary but also reading and checking the pages. Also to all the lovely people who posed for specific photos including Bapak Sita, Sita, Rehen, Faisal, Dyas, Diandra, Dio and others. Thank you to Michael Ewing for sharing his selection of photos from Java, Bali and Ambon. A big thank you to Michelle Purwagani in Surabaya for allowing the use of her lovely photos (and selfies!). Also Denise Hibbs, Alan Hibbs, Aden Hibbs Bridge, Barb Slee, Anna Sutiyono, Michael Purwagani (and Mary and Ronny), Wendy Miller, Tracey Ferguson and Irene Ritchie for their photos. Thank you to Indonesian language and linguistic experts Stuart Robson and Urip Sutiyono for their clarification on word choice, and Yayuk Sutiyono for being there all those years ago! To Asita Majdi and husband Faisal in Yogyakarta, a big thank you and appreciation for recording all the Indonesian language audio. Thank you also to my patient and supportive editor in Singapore, June Chong, and Simon Markom (PT Java Books Indonesia) for his careful and considered checking of specific Indonesian words and phrases at the final stage. This dictionary reflects the language and rich culture of Indonesia and I hope it provides enjoyment whether you are about to visit Indonesia, hoping to expand your existing vocabulary or a senior student seeking to revise your knowledge before an exam.

"Books to Span the East and West"

Tuttle Publishing was founded in 1832 in the small New England town of Rutland, Vermont [USA]. Our core values remain as strong today as they were then—to publish best-in-class books which bring people together one page at a time. In 1948, we established a publishing office in Japan—and Tuttle is now a leader in publishing English-language books about the arts, languages and cultures of Asia. The world has become a much smaller place today and Asia's economic and cultural influence has grown. Yet the need for meaningful dialogue and information about this diverse region has never been greater. Over the past seven decades, Tuttle has published thousands of books on subjects ranging from martial arts and paper crafts to language learning and literature—and our talented authors, illustrators, designers and photographers have won many prestigious awards. We welcome you to explore the wealth of information available on Asia at www.tuttlepublishing.com.

Distributed by

North America, Latin America & Europe
Tuttle Publishing
364 Innovation Drive
North Clarendon,
VT 05759-9436 U.S.A.
Tel: 1 (802) 773-8930
Fax: 1 (802) 773-6993
info@tuttlepublishing.com
www.tuttlepublishing.com

Indonesia
PT Java Books Indonesia
Kawasan Industri Pulogadung
Jl. Rawa Gelam IV No. 9
Jakarta 13930
Tel: (62) 21 4682-1088
Fax: (62) 21 461-0206
crm@periplus.co.id
www.periplus.com

Asia Pacific
Berkeley Books Pte. Ltd.
3 Kallang Sector #04-01/02
Singapore 349278
Tel: (65) 6741-2178
Fax: (65) 6741-2179
inquiries@periplus.com.sg
www.tuttlepublishing.com

**The free online audio recordings for this book
may be downloaded as follows:**

Type the following URL into your web browser:
www.tuttlepublishing.com/Indonesian-Picture-Dictionary
For support, email us at info@tuttlepublishing.com

mie instan
instant noodles

galeri kesenian
art gallery

kain dan kebaya
a traditional batik
skirt and blouse

nangka
jackfruit

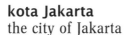

Keluarga kami naik sepeda motor.
Our family is traveling by motorbike.

bajaj
a motorised three
wheel vehicle
(Jakarta)

kota Jakarta
the city of Jakarta